ACHIEVING PROMISES

ACHIEVING PROMISES

A SPIRITUAL GUIDE
FOR THE TRANSITIONS OF LIFE

by William F. Kraft

THE WESTMINSTER PRESS
Philadelphia

BOOK DESIGN BY DOROTHY ALDEN SMITH

First edition

Published by The Westminster Press ®
Philadelphia, Pennsylvania

PRINTED IN THE UNITED STATES OF AMERICA
9 8 7 6 5 4 3 2 1

To Elizabeth and Jerry

Library of Congress Cataloging in Publication Data

Kraft, William F., 1938–
  Achieving promises.

  Bibliography: p.
  1. Christian life—Catholic authors. 2. Adulthood—Moral and religious aspects. I. Title.
BX2350.2.K65   248.8′4   81–10496
ISBN 0-664-24384-3   AACR2

CONTENTS

GRATITUDE

THANKS ARE OFFERED to the teachers, students, clients, and friends who helped me to formulate theories that, I hope, are in service of experience. Special gratitude is given to Margaret Carney, Patricia Kraft, John Krane, and the staff of The Westminster Press for taking valuable time and energy to peruse and to edit this manuscript.

Thank you Alvira Boughan, Karen Dishauzi, Sherri Fitzgerald, Ann Freggens, Bettie Gendleberg, Denise Krall, Sherel Maloney, and Debra Schneiderlochner for typing and retyping. Most of all I thank Mom, Pat, Bill, and Jennifer who patiently support me in deserts and continually invite me to dance with them in promised lands—and Dad, my friend who has run the good race and now waits for us in the Promised Land.

1

PILGRIM
PEOPLE

ALL OF US, whatever our age, are pilgrim people. We
are perpetually on our way toward our ultimate reason for being. Concretely this means that we never
arrive. If our goal is contentment, security, and happiness, we succeed only in moving along the way
toward becoming content, secure, or happy. Con-
versely we are always somewhat discontented, insecure, and unhappy. In our age when so many assume
that self-fulfillment and self-control are possible of
attainment, we have difficulty accepting life as a pilgrimage toward something ultimately beyond our
control.

Too many of us assume that adulthood is the time
when we should finally "arrive," when we should be
"grown up"—content, secure, and happy. Such a
static view, however, is inaccurate. In fact, the opposite is true. Adulthood, like childhood and adolescence, is a time of dynamic growth. The older we
become, the more we can grow up.

Studies of adult development have been sparse;

however, professional and personal interest in adult psychology has recently surged. Along with adults reflecting on their own development, a renewed interest in spiritual growth is also occurring. An increasing desire for personal spiritual meaning is strongly evident.

Original studies on spirituality and adult life-cycle development, however, are relatively rare. Popular books like those of Erikson, Sheehy, and Levinson deal mainly with the psychosocial dimensions of adulthood. With notable exceptions, recent works on adult religious development are also based on psychosocial models so that a spiritual vision is neglected.

Our pilgrimage is primarily spiritual—one that includes deserts and promised lands. Consider deserts as life crises—gifted times that pressure us to take radical stock of our lives. They present opportunities to move forward or retreat, to affirm life or deny it, to grow or stagnate. Though much has been written about psychological life crises, not much has been published on spiritual life crises. Consequently many of us find it hard to believe that seemingly barren lands can give birth to new growth as well as nourish old growth. Not many of us, for example, can accept that depression, loneliness, and anxiety—possible symptoms of dark nights—can be the necessary occasions for healthy and holy growth. Few of us recognize that absence is a necessary form of presence, that a kind of dying is essential for living.

Most of us in our Western culture assume that pain

almost always indicates something negative. Therefore we sincerely take negative stands toward what
could be positive experiences. We go through depressing times when we wonder what is "wrong"
with ourselves and never realize that such experiences could be necessary for growth. Indeed, all pain
is not symptomatic of health. It can definitely indicate pathology, and often does. Certain life-cycle
periods, however, do include discomfort. It is a popular illusion to assume that we can get to the land of
milk and honey without crossing arid and empty deserts. Rather than deceive ourselves, we are called to
accept the desert experience as necessary, particularly for spiritual growth.

Yet to declare loneliness as a good and necessary
experience to be welcomed and cultivated may
sound sick or stupid. Let us not be so sure. Spiritual
loneliness, for example, calls for deeper and more
permanent love. In loneliness we may be prepared
to experience the presence of God in his absence.
Our longing in loneliness is the condition that keeps
us growing, that makes us yearn for love—life's
Spirit.

In our healthy discontent, we strongly desire to
become more significant and creative. We seek to be
freer—to grow, to become more than we have been.
We refuse to get stuck and let life pass us by. Our life
crises mean that we can listen to the threatening but
challenging call to become more than we have been,
or we can silence its summons and regress.

Too easily we forget our spiritual side and rely too

much on that which is physical and psychosocial. Consequently we become "normally mad." We are normal insofar as we are reasonably adjusted and successful, we behave within the confines of socially sanctioned norms. Consequently we gain acceptance and earn certain rewards. Nevertheless we are mad in that we are distant from experiences that are necessary for integral (healthy) living, namely, spiritual experiences. Despite our good intentions, we become too busy to make time and give space to reflect and pray, too tired to play and love, too preoccupied to listen, too controlled to surrender, too self-sufficient to be saved.

We are programmed personally and culturally to rely exclusively on ourselves to cope with our mortality. By overstress on independence and control we find ourselves bound by our own limits. The only healthy way to cope with and transcend our limits is through "transcendent dependency," trust in God— an essential and often forgotten dynamic for spiritual growth. The spiritual life invites us to recognize and accept life as ultimately not in our hands. Love—the essential force of spiritual growth—is a gift from God which is primarily given to those who surrender to him. God, not self or others, is our saving grace. Nothing else and no one but God redeems us from absurdity and opens us to perpetual fulfillment.

Second only to love, death and dying (the "little deaths") are our most important experiences. The meaning of death in relation to spiritual development and the meaning of dying as part of living are crucial concerns not only in old age but throughout adulthood as well. I believe that creative acceptance of our own mortality evokes a transcendent appreciation of life and fosters joyful living. Throughout this book the recurrent sign of contradiction emerges: we must be willing to die in order to live.

2
A THEORY
OF SPIRITUAL LIFE-CYCLE
DEVELOPMENT

SPIRITUAL DEVELOPMENT is a perpetually dynamic process that engenders inexhaustible possibilities for growth. Knowing that "deserts" and "promised lands" are essential aspects of our spiritual journey, we can do various things to foster holy and healthy living. Instead of becoming "normal" people without spirit, we can celebrate life as people of Spirit.

This chapter presents a general view of spiritual development throughout the adult life cycle. It offers a way of looking at life—a vision that sheds light on the darkness of our understanding. My vision sheds light on the problems, challenges, and possibilities of adult pilgrims who journey through deserts on their way toward promised lands.

The method primarily is to suspend theories, beliefs, and assumptions in order to unfold the meaning of our experienced world. Specifically, we will examine the components of spiritual life-cycle growth throughout young adulthood, early adulthood, midlife, middle age, and the elderly years.

14

The vision incorporates to various degrees the findings of scholars. Particularly Jung, Bühler, Erikson, Gould, Vaillant, Levinson, Sheehy, Kimmel, Kalish, Kastenbaum, Bischof, and Kübler-Ross have contributed to my perspective. Classic and contemporary spiritual literature also adds to our vision. Personal journeys with friends and clients have generated a concrete appreciation for and validation of life-cycle processes. Finally, my students and I have conducted and analyzed more than a thousand interviews with persons eighteen to ninety-six. The responses served as a springboard to suggest and support one theory of psychospiritual development.

A VISION OF PILGRIMAGE

Our theory poses that the whole span of life consists of a series of developmental stages, that one stage of development builds on what has gone before and leads to what is to follow. These stages are fairly predictable and each stage is linked with transitional crises—times when we are pressured to restructure life. The value of such an approach is that it can help us prepare ourselves for these stages, and engender within us a sense of support for other people going through similar experiences. Each stage consists of times of *transition, crisis,* and *implementation.*

The transition phase refers to the movement from one stage of development to another such as from young adulthood to early adulthood. Such a transition usually involves adjustment to new social and

personal expectations. It also serves as a prelude to
the forthcoming crisis. In somewhat different language, a transition can be considered to be the
threshold of a desert experience. It is a time when we
can see the desert's vast nothingness, hear its silent
voices, feel its phantom touch, smell its exotic aroma.
It can both frighten and entice. We can enter it ex-
pectantly or stop journeying and pretend the desert
is not there.

The desert experience is the crisis of spiritual development. The word comes from the Latin *serere*
(to join together) and *de* (away from). It refers to the
time when things that are normally together come
apart. Our lives come to a change of pace. Things
that had made sense now seem to make nonsense.
The time for a new season emerges. In the desert we
feel abandoned—deserted. No-thing seems to make
sense. Something or someone is radically missing. In
this spiritual crisis, the ground of our being is shaken,
and we feel anxious and helpless. Our vulnerability,
mortality, and ultimate dependency are acutely felt.
To rely primarily on our own powers is simply inadequate. We realize we cannot save ourselves. Being
stripped of our normal supports and standing naked
in a dry and barren land, we yearn for deliverance.

Frequently God seems to be absent precisely
when we feel we need him most. Recoiling in an-
guish, we dread the prospects of a lonely passion.
Consciously or unconsciously, we ask God to take this
Gethsemane away, but our plea seems to be unheard.
To follow God's way especially when feeling aban-

doned is the ultimate test. If we creatively accept our desert journey, we come to experience God's saving presence in his apparent absence. No longer do we futilely try to save ourselves from oblivion. We can leap in faith beyond our limited selves and lay hold of the unlimited resources of God's Spirit. We can say: not me, but you, O Lord.

An understanding of time and its relation to life and death is crucial also to our vision. We use two meanings of time: *chronos* and *kairos*. *Chronos* refers to quantifiable "clock time." Technically it corresponds to the modern notion of time as a series of isolated moments. Living only according to chronological time, we futilely strive to live for the present as if our past and our future were not at stake. We live frantically as if there is no tomorrow and no life after death. Although such a life is busy, it is not dynamic. Such a static view impedes a dynamic vision of the aging experience and can engender a weary and depressing outlook.

Kairos refers to sacred time, to occasions when the regularity of our chronotic time breaks down allowing more significant and transcendent experiences to break in upon us. Kairotic time is qualitative and gratuitous rather than quantitative and controlled. It is a gifted time, an opportune time, a time that embraces and transcends all seasons and ages. It is a sacred time, a time for the presence of God.

Both modes of time are necessary and desirable. The scheduled time of *chronos* is needed for functional order and productivity. Even more significantly, it can be used to serve and foster the more important and life-giving time of *kairos*. Spiritual deserts as well as promised lands are rich in the possibility of kairotic events that break in upon us. Such events pressure us to reevaluate our use of all time in order to be more open and responsive to spiritual living.

Sacred events redeem us from the boredom of our daily grind. Inspired by the Spirit, our everyday lives become enthusiastic, our psychosocial functioning becomes easier, and our service to others becomes more productive and meaningful. In fact, our entire life improves when we experience the saving Spirit in the desert experience of *kairos*.

Listen to Charles Cummings: "In the desert experience of God's absence we can meet him in hidden forms; his desert presence and transforming power are concealed by a cloud that only a vision of faith and love can penetrate. . . . The desert experience is our spiritual purification for a new life of freedom and love in the land that God will show us." (*Spirituality and the Desert Experience*, pp. 22–23.)

Faith, hope, and love are always critical for salvation, especially in the desert. From our human perspective, faith is seen as a creative acceptance of experience that cannot be rationally explained. In faith, we embrace God's presence or absence. In hope, we wait in ready expectation for God's Spirit. In love, we receive and give the Spirit of life that affirms and fosters community.

A spiritual crisis is a time when we reevaluate life.

We come to a crossroad and can move deeper into or farther away from authentic living. We can face reality and through some pain become more mature, happier, and enthusiastic. Or we can run from reality, benumb our sensitivity, and repress the radical questions that call for crucial responses. Crisis is a decisive time that results in progress, fixation, or regression. Such turning points can occur at any time; however, certain crises occur because of life-cycle development. Life-cycle changes are times of crises or deserts. We neither create nor control the desert; rather, the desert is a graced time beyond our control that invites us to become more than we are.

In desert times, the meaning of life is put into question. We are thrown back on ourselves and asked to take stock. We find ourselves on center stage with only ourselves to face, and classical questions emerge. Who am I? Where am I going? From whence do I come? Death, work, play, sex, suffering, faith, hope, and love are brought into question. Coming face-to-face with the essential meaning of life is a spiritual issue of major magnitude.

When we feel that our world is coming apart we can be tempted to look for some magical miracle to save us. Our thesis is that we must be purified and emptied in the desert, become more intimate with God and be fulfilled by him, to become more than we can be on our own.

The journey through the desert is necessary to reach the promised land. However, there are perils and temptations in the desert as well. Desert demons

entice us to seek power, pleasure, or self-idolatry as
a way to escape our helplessness, pain, and dependency. False promises seduce us. Rather than trust-
ing God, we depend on ourselves. In this way the
desert provides the occasion of our undoing.

After transitional crisis experience, we come to a
time of implementation. Now we settle down and
live according to the values found in the desert or
those which result from a denial of the desert. The
way we live depends highly upon our lived remem-
brance and experience of kairotic time. In contrast to
the more critical times of transition, the process of
implementation is relatively stable and secure. We
emerge from being pulled apart in the desert to
come together with ourselves and others in a land of
promise. We come from creative chaos to creative
order. Our suffering Lent leads to a joyful Easter.

Perhaps more precisely, the promised lands of
growth are more on the order of oases. *The* Promised
Land toward which we continually journey is actually the place where and the time when we will experience total and permanent fulfillment. It is the Kingdom of God. We are on earth, however, not in
heaven. We are never completely fulfilled and
happy, never without suffering and unrest. We are
pilgrims who seek to experience the Kingdom. Life
is a rhythmic journey through deserts and oases until
we finally arrive at our destiny. Death is the final
transition from the ultimate desert on earth; we hope
that it is to the final Promised Land in heaven.

Thus, adult development is an ongoing process of

transition and implementation. We move from a relatively stable and familiar land into an upsetting and foreign desert, where we confront radical and critical issues. If we emerge from the desert in a healthy way, we again come to a more settled mode of living.

How we handle these changes can vary considerably. For instance, the transitional phase that usually evokes anxiety can lead to denial, anger, or escape. Or it can fill us with anxious fascination and anticipation of new growth. While in a desert we can feel depressed and hopelessly lost; however, deserts can become familiar and welcome places, where in silence we hear more and in darkness we expand our vision. The life-building phase of implementation can also be positive, negative, or both. Indeed, there is danger in becoming complacent instead of vigilant in building structures that promote growth. Illusory contentment can cause us to forget who we are and to lose our spirit.

Within this pattern of development the following stages can be identified:

YOUNG ADULTHOOD (ages 18–29)
    transition from adolescence (ages 18–19)
    crisis of young adulthood (ages 19–22)
    period of implementation (ages 22–29)

EARLY ADULTHOOD (ages 29–39)
    transition from young adulthood (ages 29–30)
    crisis of early adulthood (ages 30–32)
    period of implementation (ages 32–39)

MID-LIFE ADULTHOOD (ages 39–49)
   transition from early adulthood (ages 39–40)
   mid-life crisis (ages 40–42)
   period of implementation (42–49)

MIDDLE-AGED ADULTHOOD (ages 49–64)
   transition from mid-life adulthood (ages 49–50)
   crisis of middle age (ages 50–52)
   period of implementation (ages 52–64)

ELDERLY ADULTHOOD (age 64 to death)
   transition from middle-aged adulthood (ages 64–65)
   crisis of the elderly years (ages 65–72)
   period of implementation (age 72 to death)

Considerable debate exists among psychologists of adulthood concerning whether or not predictable life crises actually occur. Some researchers contend that life-cycle crises do not necessarily occur, while others hold that crises occur but at nonspecific times. The third group is convinced that crises occur at fairly predictable times.

Although our approach is based on the school of sequential development, we do not minimize the research of the other two schools, nor do we absolutize our own truth. Admittedly some people may not experience life-cycle crises for various reasons. Whatever generalizations we may draw about adults, we know that not all people grow spiritually in a rhythmic way—through deserts and promised lands.

Our proposed age ranges can vary considerably.

The standard deviation from the norm is much larger in adults than standard deviations in children and adolescents. The purpose of using age ranges is to point to general trends that are useful in making the theory concrete. They also enable one to compare oneself with others, and to prepare for one's own desert experiences. Kairotic crises do not strictly follow a chronological schedule; still, most of us are likely to experience significant change within or close to the age parameters. These age ranges do not indicate how long the phases last for every individual, for there can be considerable variability from person to person.

It is our contention that spiritual growth is primarily sequential and dynamic. Its stages and phases build on and influence one another. For instance, fixation in one stage of development will influence all subsequent stages; a particular difficulty with one stage may engender regression to a more comfortable stage. On the other hand, healthy acceptance of pain and growth possibilities in one stage facilitates acceptance and growth in others and often makes future desert journeys easier. Desert crises are not necessarily excruciating, but they are "critical" in the sense of fostering or impeding growth. A key to healthy, holy growth is to accept creatively life's settled and critical times—to face the present in faith and love, to look to the future in trust and hope, and to celebrate the past in gratitude and praise.

3

YOUNG ADULTHOOD

"So, YOU'RE GOING TO GRADUATE from high school this year. That's really great. What are you going to do? Where are you going to live? Are you going to college? Which one? Do you have a major? Who's going to pay for it? Do you have a summer job? What do your parents think? You're lucky. Good luck!

"Oh, you're not going to college. Why not? What are you going to do? How are you going to live? Do you have a job? Is it a good one? What about a career? Don't join the service. Don't get married. Make money. Travel. Get established. Live it up. Take your time. But don't waste time. Are you moving away from home? Who is going to help your parents? Be careful, it's a hard life. But you're young. You're really lucky. The best of luck!"

These questions reveal the pressure of expectations typical of the transition from late adolescence to young adulthood. A bit before or soon after high school graduation, "late" adolescents enter a new era. They experience significant environmental and social changes involving new role expectations. These young people feel the uncomfortable but exciting transition between not quite being young adults and no longer being adolescents. Late adolescents stand on the brink of young adulthood.

The work or school dilemma presents new opportunities as well as tests one's ability to cope under stress. For instance, entering the world of either work or higher education exposes one to different socioeconomic backgrounds, different ethnic groups and races, as well as new educational, recreational, and travel experiences. All of these evoke value confrontations and the need for value clarification. The adjustment to leaving home and entering a new living situation tests one's coping mechanisms that previously have been taken for granted. Some young adults experience difficulties in studying or adjusting socially, even though they had little difficulty before. Most, however, manage to make the necessary adjustments when they should be made.

DESERT OF DISCOVERY

Most of us between the ages of nineteen and twenty-two experience what might be called the crisis of young adulthood. It is a time when we confront ourselves and radically reevaluate the meaning of our lives. We ask crucial questions of ourselves: Who am I? Where am I going? What is life all about?

It is a time when adolescent values are questioned and modified; when everything and everyone, including oneself, is thrown into question. In the desert of young adulthood, nothing much makes sense. No particular thing is as fulfilling or meaningful as it was in the recent past. Instead of accepting answers, the focus now is on asking questions and criticizing answers. The meanings life had for us recede into the background. We must find new ways to affirm our identity so we may surrender, share, and commit ourselves to something that makes sense. What is important? To what ends does one choose and act? Such questions are essential to spiritual growth, for if our values and commitments are unexamined, we are likely to live a shallow and meaningless life. This special time beckons us to question our values.

Though not yet "adults," we are on our way to finding our pace and place in life. Paradoxically, out of feeling that we are "no one" living "nowhere," we actually become more mature. It is not easy, however, to journey through this desert, particularly if we are used to getting what we want when we want it. The desert experience challenges the life of indulgence and calls for discipline. What is needed is the self-discipline that makes us truly free.

Our desert journey is lonely. On cold and quiet nights, we hear, deep within ourselves, questions: Can I give to and receive from another? Will I ever be genuinely intimate with another person? With whom? Where? How? When? We reach out but our touch falls short. We speak but no one hears. We listen but we hear nothing.

Because of past interpersonal experiences, we may

be frightened to death of what we want most—intimacy. Or we may simply feel helpless or ignorant about how to know people. We may discover that we feel misunderstood and unknown; perhaps because we hide from others, feeling unworthy and ashamed to offer ourselves. Whatever the situation, we can hear our silent screams for love. We yearn for the healing presence of another person. Though we may feel afraid, helpless, or unworthy, we want to reach out; to touch and to be touched.

Loneliness is essential to coming to love. It purifies us for the gift of one another and ultimately for God. In and through loneliness, we not only become aware of ourselves so we can share ourselves more fully and deeply with others; but also we begin to realize, often unconsciously, that God is at the center of our lives. In the yearning silence of loneliness, we can hear whispers of a divine call.

Self-confrontation in loneliness is a crisis of loving and ultimately of being loved. In this advent of love, we ask ourselves: Can I love myself? Can I love another? Can I live the true spirit of life—love? Am I worthy of love? Can I be loved no matter what? Does love exist for me? Will I always be lonely? Will my questions ever be answered? Without such questions, without such dark nights of loneliness, it is difficult and perhaps impossible to live an authentic life of love.

Without love, life becomes bland and listless, lacking in enthusiasm and spirit. The paradox is that as young adults we must travel the desert of loneliness

to enjoy the lands of love. The ever-present dangers
are to accept counterfeits of love or to numb ourselves in the pain of self-discovery. Escapes from
loneliness are available, numerous, and tempting.
Sex, work, and drugs, for instance, can silence the
summons of loneliness so that love is forgotten in
service of fatal comfort.

No longer adolescent and not yet adult engenders
anxiety that can lead one into general spiritual
growth. When we question our values, beliefs, and
principles, we can feel left without anything, in a
nowhere land, feeling like nobody. Feeling lost and
wondering if we have anything or anyone to hold on
to can be an opportunity and an invitation to empty
ourselves for more than self. The opportunity can be
foreclosed by attempting to fill the emptiness ourselves without listening for God to speak.

A common danger is to judge our feelings as negative. The result is that we feel guilty about conditions
that are psychologically and spiritually healthy.
Rather than accepting these feelings, we repress
them, or seek to escape from them, or try to numb
our awareness of them. To combat such negative
attitudes we must cultivate discipline. However, to
delay immediate satisfaction in service of healthier
fulfillment can seem senseless for people who have
always had their needs satisfied. In our self-centered
striving for pleasure, we find it most difficult to re-
strain our own desires. On the other hand, some
young adults really do repress experiences. Instead
of "letting it all hang out" or doing what they feel,

they hold their feelings and desires "in" and feel guilty for doing their thing. Neither the life of license nor the life of restriction is likely to lead to health and fulfillment.

Spiritual as well as psychological stress challenges our mental health. Either can activate latent problems. If through childhood and adolescence latent processes have been held in check, they are likely to emerge at this time. For instance, those who are basically compulsive may become more compulsive under the stress of spiritual change. Or consider persons who come from an overly protective home. Uprooting and crisis can leave them so precariously on their own that they fail to cope. Others, however, may become stronger and healthier because of the way they respond to the challenge.

Another danger is to become extremely "independent" as a reaction to the natural and healthy dependency most adolescents experience. As an attempt to free ourselves from family dependence, we try to live completely on our own. Physical and social independence, however, does not guarantee psychological and spiritual independence. In fact, mature independence includes a certain kind of dependence wherein we freely choose to be interdependent.

Since we are embodied people, our spiritual and psychological changes are manifest in various physical ways. Sometimes we dress differently as a way of showing our new being in the world. Or we may manifest some change in manners or behavior. Keep in mind that psychosomatic changes may indicate healthy, though stressful, growth and not necessarily illness.

In the desert away from the marketplace, we realize that spiritual life has to do with discovering our authentic place in the world. We discover that to feel radically worthwhile, no matter what occurs, depends more on our spiritual roots than on our social status. Social pressures upon the young adult to succeed, to settle down, to accept privileges like voting, and responsibilities like paying taxes, can obscure and short-circuit the learning opportunities of the desert.

Conventional morality should be questioned and challenged, even more deeply than in adolescence. Rather than conforming to rules and expectations of society just because they are conventional, we may become acutely aware of individual rights and values that are prior to social systems and even to personal attachments. This period of questioning is often part of the process that leads to a "post-conventional" stand toward morality, a stand which, according to Lawrence Kohlberg, few adults attain. Too many remain conventional, following the law rather than listening to its spirit. Others seize upon a self-servicing morality—doing what feels "good." Yet another approach is to regress to an earlier mode of morality when under pressure or faced with responsibility. For instance, young adults who become parents often regress to what they previously criticized—their parents' "old-fashioned and authoritarian morals."

Some adults come to the final stage of cognitive

normal development, the "universal ethical principle level," around the age of twenty-one. It is emphasized, however, that an authentic morality is not primarily a function of cognitive development. Basically it is a spiritual process. Thus, the way a spiritual crisis is resolved makes a significant impact on the development of morality.

Conflict between morals and mores also erupts. We become acutely aware of the differences in norms for good behavior. For example, if a young woman values celibacy and yet under pressure apologizes for being celibate, she is caught between contending values. It is difficult to live with integrity especially when our subculture, reference group, or community holds morals that differ from our own. It takes courage and conviction to live by one's standards regardless of the presence or absence of environmental support.

There are several popular ways to resolve moral conflict. One is the way of "relativism." We say that everything is relative (depending on situational factors) and that nothing is objective or absolute. (We fail to realize that this principle is an objective absolute.) A view offers the test of "honesty and sincerity," which posits that as long as one is honest and sincere, the behavior is good. (We can forget that sin can be honest and sincere.) Some young adults try to become amoral, often implying that reason can handle everything and that guilt is an unnecessary impediment. The moral imperative is to be without moral scruples.

Most young desert travelers also question religion. Some of us become quite critical of religious institutions, their practices, and their members. Young adults are especially critical of phoniness, double standards, and ready-made solutions. In reaction "we" may become agnostic and doubt everything, or we may try out new religions. Actually, most young adults want to be touched by religion, desiring it to be experiential rather than just theoretical, to be fulfilled with love rather than with ideas.

Along with criticizing religion, young adults often question notions of God. God may become more absent than present. Some take a humanistic position rather than a spiritual one, stating that life can be authentically meaningful without a transcendent God. Life's meaning is totally in our hands. A popular illusion is to try to become indifferent to any religious quest by regarding religion as a dead issue. We seriously hurt ourselves when we stop seeking truth; rather, we should continue our questioning, for it leads to an appreciation of the sacred.

In seeking a mature stand, many young adults find themselves immersed in a multitude of views. Many were raised without clear values, or to think that all views are equal, or to assume that what feels comfortable is always good or right. Instead of having a strong value system to criticize and explore, they are left with nothing to examine. Dialogue becomes silent and growth is consequently stunted. They are left with nothing but themselves—a painfully isolated and narcissistic position.

Another key issue in spiritual growth is what it means to be a man or a woman. What is the relationship of sex to gender and how to integrate them? Who am I? And who can I be? are both spiritual as well as sexual questions.

Spiritual processes also evoke questions about genital sex. For instance, what approach does a young adult take toward genital feelings? Repress them? Satisfy them? Can they really be integrated? How? Increasingly more young adults and adolescents as well are likely to satisfy their needs. Few know how to relate sexuality to spirituality. Some young adults postpone such issues, and others, though not as many as in the past, repress their genital feelings. Increasingly, however, more satisfy them prematurely and unauthentically. Not many bring genitality into harmony with their psychosocial-spiritual selves to become whole persons.

Besides reaching their genital peak, many men tend to maximize genital sexuality while minimizing the other more basic aspects of sexuality—feelings that lead to intimacy but not necessarily to genital sex. Furthermore, beginning in childhood many young men have been taught to assume that affective feelings are only in service of genital sexuality. Thus, young men may have problems in expressing affective sexuality as an end in itself—without somehow leading to genital satisfaction. Such sexual programming is a serious obstacle to spiritual growth. It often inhibits intimate sharing and love. Although young women in the past were taught to experience affec-

tive sexuality as an end in itself, contemporary
women more freely use affection as an end, or as a
means to genital sexuality. Thus, many women are
freer than men in expressing affection, which is usually a positive, though often frustrating, factor in
their spiritual lives.

Among the main obstacles to spiritual health—the
desert demons—are negative injunctions from self
and others. Frequently we are made to feel guilty for
positive and necessary feelings. For instance, it is
difficult to feel lonely without some sense of guilt,
and it is common to feel depressed about being depressed. Too often we are left alone without help, or
we seek help that impedes. Other negative forces
include peer pressure to take drugs or to indulge in
sex. More socially sanctioned obstacles include escaping into marriage or becoming overly busy.

Spiritual growth, which includes pain and joy, simply is not congruent with many cultural norms.
Young people are expected to be vital and "happy"
—without a care in the world. To feel loneliness as a
prelude to deeper love is seldom accepted. To experience depression in the service of fulfillment is rejected; only fulfillment without emptiness is accepted. In many ways, we impede healthy and holy
growth when we are seduced by well-intentioned,
but negative approaches, such as trying to purge ourselves of anxiety and loneliness which may contrib-
ute to health.

It is prudent to realize, however, that it is rare and
perhaps impossible to be without any "demons"—

forces that militate against healthy and holy growth. Rather than trying to kill our demons, we should understand their devious ways, and consequently and paradoxically become stronger because of the encounter. In other words, we combat madness with sanity, and we confront our demons with good spirits. When we forget that we are sinners who need to be saved, we risk damnation.

In escaping and transcending negative forces, a good home and an understanding family are important aids. If parents are closed or unavailable, a mature brother or sister, a relative, or a friend should be sought. The person who understands and appreciates our world can help us lessen the pain and increase the joy of becoming young adults.

With or without family and friends, a trustworthy mentor usually plays a significant role in young adulthood. Ideally, our primary mentors have been, and continue to be, our parents. Other mentors such as a teacher, supervisor, counselor, "older" friend, or relative can crucially influence the way we develop. The good mentor is primarily a person who witnesses to holy and healthy attitudes, who follows a wholesome life-style, and who encourages, supports, and inspires us to become our authentic selves. Our challenge is to choose and cultivate mentors of the heart as well as of the mind. Academic and professional mentors will consciously or unconsciously guide our intellectual and functional pursuits and successes. The spiritual mentor, however, is paramount in the ongoing formation of the spiritual life and conse-

quent holiness and happiness. With the help of a
mentor, we novices of adulthood can learn to become our true selves rather than become caricatures
of authentic adulthood.

It is wise to be patient, but in our times of immediate satisfaction, patience is a lost art. As young adults
we have time to bear the pain to self-emergence, and
to wait in the desert for the promised land of fulfillment. Instead of going too quickly, or experiencing
too much too soon, we can and should go slowly. We
can take time to explore, experience, and travel; to
meet various kinds of people; and especially to discover ourselves. Taking time for solitude, as in any
life passage, is crucial in coming to discover and be
oneself. Reading good literature affirms and clarifies
the confusion and darkness of self-emergence. A personal journal in which we hover daily over experiences in order to increase self-awareness can also be
helpful. The advent of adulthood calls for a prudent
and patient journey in faith.

LAND OF SURRENDER

The period of implementation, though not without
stress, is a relatively stable and settled time in contrast to the crisis of transition. Life usually comes
together for better or worse. For most of us, it is the
time when we begin our professional and personal
vocations. Although these decisions are not irrevoca-
ble, they do make a significant impact on our future
lives. Fortunately most of us can afford to take our

time rather than commit ourselves prematurely. We have the time and energy to explore various types of social involvement, and to try different jobs. We also have freedom from many restraints and the freedom for many possibilities. It is the time to explore and master the world. The functional dimension of living is stressed, and the focus is on coping with the external world and succeeding in it.

Along with exploration, there is often a trend toward more conservative and traditional values, perhaps because of social responsibilities and career expectations and the pressure to function successfully. As young adults we are pressured to learn to adjust to the world. We learn to be "normative adults," to learn to implement the roles of worker, citizen, socializer, community member, spouse, parent, helper, friend.

Young adulthood is the time when we are challenged to live commitments and values that shape our lives. The way we implement them depends highly on how we have managed the time of transition. If we aborted the crisis, we are unlikely to live a spiritual and integral life-style. Even if we have come to an authentic stand, we can easily become overinvolved with social and economic responsibilities and forget to nourish our spiritual selves. A common error is to measure our worth by our material possessions and social status. This militates against spiritual growth. Climbing up the economic and social ladder may well mean a diminution of spirituality. It is easy to be seduced by the madness that minimizes and rationalizes spiritual living.

Communal living is a strong test of our commitment and values. For example, a strong or weak marital foundation is usually built in young adulthood. The prudent young couple realize that they must consistently practice love; otherwise, they can simply adjust and forget to love. Other realities such as children, work, and financial problems also test us. Members of a religious community soon learn the difference between their "spiritual honeymoon" and the humdrum of everyday living.

Living in love is a concrete test of integrating that which is functional and that which is spiritual. Do we express or repress the meaning of "suffering love"? Ideally, we begin to foster an unconditional love— learning to love without expectation of return. We learn that love is not primarily a matter of satisfying or adjusting our feelings. Real love goes beyond these physical and psychosocial dimensions to a more lasting and fulfilling experience. We must learn to express love, not only with friends and spouse but also with children who cannot return the same kind of love that we give. How to cultivate love day to day is a key factor in developing an authentic spiritual life. The danger is to become too absorbed with the functional grind of living and neglect the spiritual core of our existence. The challenge is to function in ways that are congruent with and foster love.

Friendship can also be an important element for spiritual growth. To be understood and appreciated in more than functional ways can give needed courage to pursue the spiritual life. Such friendship can help us to accept and transcend the problems that inevitably evolve in living spiritually. It can also give us support and help to nourish our spiritual selves at a time that demands us to be highly functional.

Expectations, however, of how men and women should act and look can also impede our spiritual growth. Young men, for example, can be so busy in their work that they forget to nourish their affective and spiritual lives. The relatively minimal influence of women in the political and industrial worlds as well as in institutional religion can be reinforced rather than challenged in young adulthood. Accepting a minimal role for women contributes to a one-sided masculine society and church. Also consider how each sex views itself. A man usually centers his self-esteem too much around work, while a woman centers her life around serving others. Becoming too functional, we begin to withdraw from the spiritual life. Consequently we lose contact with the original and ultimate source of our worth.

Toward the end of young adulthood we can probably look back on milestones, such as personal vocation, parenthood, and career choice. These kinds of milestones are important. Yet our challenge is to integrate them with our spiritual lives. Without spiritual values, life becomes a sham and a hell. Job and service may lead to success without permanent meaning. Forgetting the Spirit of life blinds us to beautiful visions, silences mystical music. It stops joyful rhythms, suppresses pleasant aromas, blunts delectable tastes, aborts peaceful rest.

As young adults we can fool ourselves by assuming that we have plenty of time to change our lives. We may live as if we have innumerable possibilities to do what we want. Living in the illusion of inexhaustible time, we can take life and love for granted. In our naive optimism we can forget to nourish our spiritual lives. As "free spirits" we can fail to develop structures for our growth in freedom. Consequently we can slowly and unknowingly lose our spirit.

Thus, it behooves us to promote the interior life instead of being too outer-directed, to be vigilant in setting structures that foster spiritual growth. Rather than succumbing to social and cultural pressure to value *having* over *being* and function over spirit, life should center on becoming primarily and ultimately spiritual. Instead of slowly falling out of love particularly in pursuit of success, our challenge is to grow in love—to surrender spiritually.

4

EARLY ADULTHOOD

BY THE END of our third decade, most of us are able to cope with demands, responsibilities, and overall pressures. Many of us also have gained satisfaction from our work and may have enjoyed the taste of success. But just when life seems set, we begin to look again at the past and wonder about the future. We get the uncomfortable feeling that the "honeymoon" will soon end and a new desert looms on the horizon.

As in earlier transitions, we experience new expectations from self and others. People again begin to look at us differently and expect different behavior from us. We feel the pressure to "act adult"—to be sober, settled, and sane. No longer do we have quite the same freedom to be silly, unsettled, and "weird." At work or play, we feel more the need to be responsible. Our transition from young adulthood ushers in the desert of early adulthood.

Though we may have been somewhat aware of becoming older, we are likely to feel it now in a new and disturbing way. We will be aware of youth slip-

ping away when we reach the mythical age of
twenty-nine. We are pressured to admit that soon we
will no longer be young, but rather, "mature." We
are people who are neither young nor old; not yet in
the middle years, but people who have been seasoned. Unsettling as it may be, we are faced with the
fact that the last vestiges of youth have slipped away.

DESERT OF SELF-CONCERN

Questions! Questions! Questions! Just when our life
was becoming orderly, something again unsettles it.
After the busy years we spent establishing ourselves
as young adults, a new crisis may come as a surprise
or seem unfair. We may feel that we should be settled by now; nevertheless we again question life.
Whom have I become? Do I want the next ten years
to be like the past ten? Am I phony? What are my
goals? What are my values? Is this all there is? In
short: I focus on "me."

To be concerned for ourselves is a healthy process
that challenges us to grow not just for ourselves but
for others as well. A lack of personal freedom dimin-
ishes our presence to and for others. We are called to
be more responsible for ourselves, which enables us
to be more responsible to others. There is a peril of
egotism and excessive self-centeredness that is to be
avoided. On the other hand a proper respect for oneself is a healthy and necessary basis for respect for
others. We can feel unnecessary guilt that impedes
our self-discovery. Rather than being an exercise in

psychological narcissism, our desert of self-concern is a necessary part of our spiritual growth. It behooves us to abstain from guilt and to have the courage to change. Instead of assuming that our feelings are exclusively self-serving, we can accept them as a necessary step in spiritual growth, being more alive for God's sake.

A main task of this period is to take stock of ourselves in order to claim our freedom—freedom from restrictions and freedom for more fulfillment. Aiming for more self-development, we look for experiences that engender self-development. In the desert of early adulthood, we focus on ourselves—on what life can give us, and what we can freely give in return. Frequently, for example, women protest against being treated mainly as a function—mother, wife, provider, servant, "second-class citizen." They strive for and demand more freedom and actualization. Listen to this woman: "I am tired of being a servant, of giving, giving, giving. I've worked for ten years without pay or much recognition. My family simply expect me to wait on them. I'm tired of being taken for granted. What about me? Who gives to me? I want more! I am more!" Rather than being selfish, this woman wants to be freer for both self and others. Actually, women often experience this crisis more acutely than men, which may mean more discomfort and growth. Regardless of gender, we are concerned about actualizing ourselves.

Everything is brought into question. How am I physically? How do I look? How do I want to look?

How do I dress? Do I dress as a young person? as an older person? What does it mean to look physically mature? While feeling the tug of aging and its impending limits, we may try harder than ever to prove ourselves physically in an attempt to hold on to youth. Though in good shape, we feel the pressure to work at staying in good shape, or feeling out of shape can be an unsettling affirmation of getting older.

We also become concerned about our personal commitments. Is our marriage as good as we initially thought it would be? Too often we find that it has dissipated rather than grown. We question our past motives. Why did I get married? Did I marry the right person? Do I still really love? What is happening to my love? Why do you love me? Who loves me? In the midst of such disruption we may think of changing our commitment. Divorce or preparing for it is common at this time. We may also think of ways to renew and to promote our marital commitment to love. If single, we can be pressured to get married or can be patronized, pitied, or subtly rejected. And if we are a member of a community, we may feel that this is the time to leave or to renew our commitment.

Women, who are especially sensitive to the restrictions of being a wife and a mother, intensely feel the one-sidedness of their lives. They often give love much more than they receive it. Women, who are taken for granted and sold short, can feel alone and lonely even in a busy house. Many begin to protest and demand more appreciation and love.

Single women who seek to be more than adequate

and who want to grow spiritually find it difficult at
this time because of prejudice against their age and
sex. The irony is that most women are reaching their
psychological and sexual peak at thirty so that in
many ways they are more than ever ready to get
married. At the same time, many courageous women
have deepened their values and spiritual lives to a
degree that intimidates many men.

Many men are so involved in their work that they
can easily make their personal commitments secondary to their job. A wife, then, is secondary at best and
marriage adjusts to mediocrity. Since man's self-concern is more likely to be channeled in work or social
activities, personal loneliness and the desire to grow
in love are not often clearly and strongly felt. Unfortunately men are programmed to minimize personal
growth and to settle for the comfort of immaturity.
Men must listen to their spirit that yearns for more
than comfort and success.

It is no surprise, therefore, that this life cycle is a
prime time for divorce. Many couples covertly agree
to an implicit divorce: to adjust (for the sake of children, economic security, or social conveniences) to a
merely functional although dying marriage. A divorce in mid-life or middle age is often decided ten
or twenty years previously. The challenge is to listen
to and act on the call to deepen the marital commitment—to foster love, the heart of marriage.

Single persons, particularly women, usually suffer
the oppression of diminishing opportunities for marriage. Women often experience sexist and ageist

prejudices that impede their free movement in pursuing an authentic marital commitment. The ugly probability is that a mature woman in her thirties will encounter few mature men eligible for marriage. To compound the situation, many men, both single and married, consider single women as lonely and desperate sex objects who can be easily exploited.

These are times in which our ego strength is tested. If we have latent psychological problems, they can emerge. Depression as well as psychosomatic illness is more likely to occur. Stress can debilitate us. Our feelings can implode and develop psychosomatic illness, or they can explode in extreme behavior. Or it is hoped that our stress challenges us to become stronger.

We also wonder about the spiritual relevance of our work, but such inventory is often implicit; that is, we do not use "spiritual language." Rather, we use terms like meaning, relevance, and value. If I am a nonpaid worker, such as a homemaker, I may wonder about the worth of my work. This is understandable in the light of society's tendency to judge the value of work according to financial criteria. We can assume that more pay means more valuable work. It is easy to doubt the worth of work in the midst of a materialistic culture.

I might ask myself if my work and spiritual life function in harmony. Does work impede or implement my spiritual values? Is my spiritual life more important than my functional life? Is my life primarily one of service so that spirituality is secondary? Do

I slavishly listen to the tick of clock time while being deaf to the kairotic time of love? Is my life so scheduled that I have little time for God? Am I so busy being useful that I am too tired to be "uselessly" present to more permanent and life-giving experiences? Can I foster experiences that are ends in themselves rather than means to other ends? Am I so intent on achieving that I lack the patience to wait for God?

Is it difficult to respond authentically to such questions? Increased financial pressures and career expectations can insiduously trap us into being dedicated workaholics. Too tired to play, too preoccupied to relax, or just a general feeling of being on a treadmill are symptoms of maximizing work and minimizing spirituality. In the desert of early adulthood, we are pressured to take stock of what meaning our work has and can have. With good intentions, we can suffocate our spiritual lives and find that the reason for our being is losing its ground.

Social roles and environmental structures are also brought into self-inventory. For example, a woman asks what it means to be a wife, mother, woman; and a man questions the meaning of being a husband, father, man. A woman at this time is especially sensitive to the problems and possibilities of role functioning. She becomes concerned about herself and her future life in contrast to exclusively serving others. Or she may feel irritated with having social activities and friends primarily oriented around her husband and his work. Feeling trapped in a social desert may evoke an urge to get out. Whatever the situation, women who become aware of their environmental restrictions and possibilities often strive to move from oppression to self-determination.

In the struggle to be freer, a danger is to minimize spiritual power and maximize social and political power. Women can minimize their own dignity and fall into a normal madness that is controlled by men. To be sure: women should have equal opportunity and be treated justly, but the key is to deepen and nourish their spiritual lives, which then become a permanent and powerful ground on which to stand and act. Otherwise, women become just as "mad" as many men.

Contrary to popular belief, at this time in life many women surpass men in genital sexuality. Women begin to peak genitally in their thirties while most men decline. Thus a husband and wife may be moving in opposite directions in sexual intimacy. When a woman desires more than a man can or wants to give, she can intimidate him particularly if she integrates her genital needs with her spiritual life. In defense, a man might cover his fear with "quick" sexual exercises according to his desire and convenience. Or he might rationalize his changing behavior, saying that he is overworked, too tired, or not in the mood.

Furthermore, women are usually more open to affective sexuality, both as an end in itself and as a means to genital sex, while men tend to view affection mainly as a means to genital gratification. Expressions of affection can threaten a man who experiences it as necessarily linked to genital sex. Feeling that he must perform genitally whenever he is intimate, he may begin to build the foundation for mid-life impotence, spiritual as well as sexual.

Most men have enough difficulty in being physically intimate without feeling pressured to engage in genital intercourse. Many withdraw from intimate relationships and compensate with functional ones. The tragedy is that while becoming functional experts, men can become spiritual dolts. Women's openness to affective intimacy as an end in itself nourishes their spiritual life, while men's tendency necessarily to link affection with genitality impedes their spiritual development. Women are less likely than men to fragment sexuality, less likely to settle for less than whole sex—to settle for less than is really possible.

Adult women, however, can easily be frustrated in both the sexual and the spiritual realm. Healthy interpersonal spirituality can too easily wane and be forgotten. If a woman is frustrated, the time is ripe for an affair. She is young enough to be "culturally attractive," has the know-how to get around, and often has more opportunity. However, this crisis of adulthood can help a woman or a man become more aware of such problems and find more constructive possibilities.

A recurrent danger is to become so busy that we forget what is essential for health. A person may be actively involved even in religion and still fail to promote spiritual growth. Often a well-intentioned life of social service displaces or impedes a direct and active spiritual life. Solitude, creative pauses, and prayer are neglected or dissociated from the rest of life so that spiritual experiences may be felt as distant or as a thing of the past. To hear the call of spirituality in a loud and busy world is difficult. It is wise to slow down, to be patient in an impatient world, and to silence words in order to listen to the Word.

In our thirties we are usually responsible for influencing the moral development of children, while most of us are questioning our own moral standards. Even "superegoless" adults, who have become morally indifferent, wonder about what is best for themselves and others, though they may seek to escape from these feelings. Others have developed an expedient moral system that can foster self-centeredness. Those who have a rigid moral system are challenged to become more flexible and understanding. It is a time that challenges our moral system, whatever it is. It is a time to deepen the spiritual foundations and grow in moral maturity.

As seasoned adults, we feel the pain of loneliness and isolation more profoundly. Single people may intensely feel the problems of loneliness. Although they may have social freedom, many lack a consistent reference group, so that they often feel like outsiders. To compound matters, to be single in the thirties evokes overconcern or prejudgments. Isn't it too bad they are single? Are single persons homosexual? What's wrong with him? What's going to happen to her? Besides being lonely, single people are often oppressed, exploited, rejected, pitied, or merely tolerated.

Being single, especially female, often means exclusion from social functions, or at best tolerated. To be one of a pair is the membership card needed to enter many social functions with approval. Finding that roads, telephone lines, and invitations travel one way, single persons get discouraged trying to get "in." Some singles look for single groups that foster social activities but seldom spiritual life. In some of these groups, women can be seen as commodities to be used. Although being used or filling up time can seem better than nothing, such spiritless activity soon becomes boring and empty.

Some celibates seek to build friendships as ways of numbing their painful yearning of loneliness. Such experiences may be needed to a degree. Yet our primary goal should not be to escape loneliness, but rather to listen to it and share this call of love. Other celibates cope with loneliness by being so busy that they have no time to listen. The healthy response to loneliness is to love others, to receive love, and to seek love ultimately from God.

The danger is to misinterpret loneliness as a clear sign to leave a committed life rather than to seek and deepen love. Failure to find healthy intimacy in religious life is likely to decrease the probability of finding intimacy in another life. It is a mistake to interpret loneliness as an urge to move away from our commitment rather than deeper into it. A dangerous assumption concerning loneliness is that people can ultimately satisfy their spiritual needs. Only God can ultimately respond to our radical call of love. Only God's Spirit can support and give us life permanently and everywhere. Only God is our common ground. Loneliness is a living reminder that we are primarily dependent on God, not on one another. Indeed, we depend on one another in many ways, especially to love one another. But that dependency, though essential, is secondary to our ultimate dependency on God.

In our thirties, we begin to realize that the absence in loneliness seeks a more permanent presence. We come to realize that loneliness is a gift that presents God to be discovered—that in absence, God is more present. Since spiritual loneliness first seeks God and then others, interpersonal (and community) relationships are precariously tenuous and they progressively dissipate in Spirit when God is forgotten. Grounded together in God, however, we can courageously strive to love unrestrictedly.

Likewise, the emptiness of spiritual depression can only be fulfilled by God. Its heavy listlessness can only be enlightened and vitalized by the Holy Spirit. Social success, economic possession, political power, and even psychological insight will not heal the depressed spirit. Though medical and psychosocial approaches can and should be used to treat medical and psychosocial depressions, these methods are inadequate for spiritual experiences. Sometimes tranquilizing and analyzing hinder the emergence of spiritual questions that ask for transcendent answers.

We are often and easily pressured to focus on issues that divert our spiritual attention. We can seek temporary satisfaction at the expense of permanent fulfillment. It is crucial to seek what is more than conventionally sought, for we can fool ourselves into thinking that our salvation lies primarily in activity, adjustment, and success rather than ultimately in nothing but God.

Love—the core of spirituality and the authentic answer to loneliness—can be deepened. Feeling the staleness of our community life, the lack of its enthusiasm, vitality, and spirit, can evoke questions that call for more meaningful answers. Where and how do I want to live the rest of my life? Can I live without interpersonal intimacy? Where can I find authentic intimacy? Is it possible to be intimate forever? Can I love? Whom? How? And most importantly: Am I loved? Though love is questioned and challenged in this crisis of adulthood, we are pressured to escape from the important questions of authentic intimacy —interpersonal spirituality. It is easy to become so busy that we forget to renew life. When we do not deepen our love, we build the foundation for a dreadfully painful mid-life crisis.

A reliable sign of our spiritual health is the quality and quantity of play. When we fall out of love, we lack the spirit for spontaneous play. Some of us give a false impression of authentic play: we look as if we are vital and happy. Still our counterfeits of love progressively violate our spirit. We pursue pleasures that give us temporary fulfillment rather than foster ongoing growth and enjoyment. Realizing only a fraction of what is possible, we stunt our growth.

Rather than whispering its message as in young adulthood, death speaks more clearly: Live! Yet many studies affirm how we in our culture seek to escape death and dying. This is tragic. The ability to face death is our saving grace. Coming to terms with death can evoke a sense of wonder that helps us take a second look at life. When we ask the question, Is this all there is? we can answer, NO—there is infinitely more!

One of the strongest desert demons will tempt us with hyperactivism. Too often we fail to slow down, rest, play, or celebrate, for we desperately try to find the meaning of life in what we do rather than in who we are. Consequently we seldom take time to celebrate the mystery of being alive, and when we do have time, we become frightened and anxious. Holidays become so hectic that we are glad when they are over. We numb ourselves with alcohol. We become obsessed with activity. Life becomes a matter of adjusting to and coping with an unending series of demands. Relatively early in life when we still have many years to live, we already feel weary and discouraged. Celebration and enjoyment of life have been crowded out.

Another demon is the social pressure to succeed. A reinforced mode of normal madness seeks to gain everything and ends up with nothing. We can be unconsciously programmed to strive after mere achievement and fall far short of integral fulfillment. This false promise of happiness results in controlled despair.

To tame these desert demons and promote spiritual growth, particularly at this time, we should take creative pauses to listen to and reflect on our lives. It helps to take stock of our interpersonal spirituality. How is our life of love really lived? How can it be improved? Reflective reading, listening in solitude, and consistently loving are always ways to promote spiritual growth. Rather than becoming hyperactive and taking the ultimate meaning of life and others for granted, we can learn to appreciate and enjoy one another. Realizing that love does not grow automatically, we can set structures to practice the daily art of loving. We can structure time and space for genuine play rather than workism, for self-determination rather than dependency, for growth rather than mere adjustment, for passionate joy rather than contentment, for a life of Spirit rather than living vicariously.

LAND OF SELF-ACTUALIZATION

The rhythm of differentiation and integration, life and death, birth and rebirth goes on perpetually. For most seasoned adults, life again begins to settle in the thirties. Though not void of transitional and critical moments, this is primarily a time to restructure what was uprooted. Daniel J. Levinson points out that this is a "boom" time—becoming one's own man. (*The*

Seasons of a Man's Life, pp. 144–149.) It can also be a settling time of becoming one's stable self.

Most of us increase in power and responsibility along with a desire to make a mark on the world. Psychosocially it is a time of productive activity, or according to Erik Erikson, a time of generativity or stagnation (*Identity: Youth and Crisis,* pp. 138–139), a time when we strive to make things happen at work, in social transactions, and in our personal lives. In our thirties, we tend to "go out" rather than focus on interior journeys.

By this time most of us have solidified attitudes. Spirituality has become paramount (in experience as well as in thought) or it has become secondary, repressed, displaced, forgotten. Married couples have grown in their commitment, moved out of love, or have learned to adjust to a decaying relationship. Some singles have decided to live with someone, while others live alone, and a few have freely vowed a celibate life.

By now, we have made decisions that highly influence our present and future functional and personal lives. Many married women have taken a new stand toward their domestic responsibilities. Many plan to engage in extra domestic activities. Some women may get involved in liberation causes, others in social and political activities, religious functions, or educational pursuits. Those who do not join a group or engage in an "outside" activity are still likely to explore their "inner" freedom such as by reading and personal reflection. There are also women who repress their awareness and adjust to frustration and fragmented lives.

Unfortunately too many of us have learned to adjust to a life with minimal love. The thriving thirties can result in a mad adjustment to a spiritless life, particularly in the light of the pressure to succeed. Rather than a time to fall out of love, it is a time to share equally, to accept limits in self and others, and to strengthen our bonds with one another. We can learn to accept and celebrate our being in a perpetually imperfect community.

When we center our lives around values that foster love, our lives change. Rather than choosing friends who are only useful for professional and social climbing, we spend more time with our community. Instead of withdrawing from our spouse, we become closer—reaffirming and deepening our primary commitment. Paradoxically, our desert concern for self leads to other-centeredness.

In a healthy relationship, as men and women we share ourselves with mutual respect. As we learn from and enjoy one another more, we begin to feel freer to take on the attributes of the other sex. Women particularly assert their spirit, tolerate less oppression, and pursue a freer and more integral life. Men, however, too often become slaves to work and the pursuit of success, and their spirit becomes contained and passionless.

Instead of being a frantic time of activism and

work, early adulthood can be an optimum time for play. For most of us, it is the last time for boundless physical energy and vigor. We are still young enough to engage in vigorous physical activities. In fact, we may be at our physical peak, along with having the know-how and desire to play with zest and freedom. Our challenge is to see life as a free banquet for feasting.

If we have not resolved our crisis positively, we can continue to escape from spiritual growth, especially in overactivity manifested in workism and in compensatory pleasure. Rather than evoking life, death promises annihilation. Death becomes the opposite of life—total absurdity—and life becomes a frantic and fruitless attempt to live authentically.

If our crisis has been resolved positively, death is not denied but is listened to as a source of life. We take time out to listen, and to reflect on it, and our awareness and acceptance of death encourages us to live fully. Listening to death also helps us to listen to the death of others and consequently to appreciate them more. Knowing that our parents are coming closer to death enables us to appreciate them and enjoy them more than ever. Being in touch with death helps us to slow down and to take time to monitor life so that its Spirit does not pass us by. Death also affirms our radical helplessness—that life is not totally or even primarily in our hands. Death humbles us.

Solitude, spiritual reading, consistent interpersonal growth, are ways to combat the many obstacles of growth. We can slow down to listen to, to appreciate, and to enjoy the beauty of life and its people. Rather than forgetting the heart of life, we can be vigilant in guarding and proclaiming life's Spirit.

5

MID-LIFE
ADULTHOOD

MID-LIFE ADULTHOOD has recently become a popular topic. Most of the research has been concerned with the physical and psychosocial dimensions of mid-life. Our approach is to accent its spiritual dimension and to offer guidelines for continual learning and growth during this often frightening and life-changing period.

In our schema, mid-life is the time between early adulthood and middle age, or between ages thirty-nine and forty-nine. Although in mid-life we are not yet middle-aged, we are past the halfway point of life. At times we realize that we probably have less time to live than we have already lived, so the focus is no longer on growing up.

Many mid-life issues center around the experience of limits. As these enclose us they challenge us to seek deeper dimensions in life. Instead of evoking depression, regression, or escapism, the experience of limits is an opportunity to encounter the Unlimited. As the finitude of time calls forth the timeless, so the ultimate limit—death—renews life and generates the Infinite.

As we approach forty, we begin to reflect upon our own personal history. It may be uncomfortable to realize that high school graduation occurred more than twenty years ago. We reflect on our past dreams, goals, and ideals; how have they been fulfilled or unfulfilled? We question again. Have my personal and professional goals been reached? Have I truly lived according to my values and ideals? Have I grown? Am I growing? Have I made a significant contribution to life? Have I stopped dreaming?

Whatever our previous doubts about reaching adulthood, at forty there is no doubt about it. Most of us feel that we are slowing down, feeling less energetic than in the past. Keeping in shape, for example, may be much more work than play. At times we feel too tired to cope with new pressures. We already have many personal and social responsibilities, and we are reluctant to commit time and energy to enter a new time of transition and trial. The promise of change threatens our life-style, and some of us prefer to stay at "thirty-nine."

At the threshold of this desert, we can hear the faint but clear voice of the noonday devil. Our contained spirits cry out for truth. Death can be seen lurking in the distant shadows, seeking a confrontation, perhaps mocking us, trying to intimidate us so we withdraw from the desert. Now is the time we need courage to enter the desert to face and trans-

cend our limited selves, to answer the demon of
death with life.

DESERT OF LIMITS

The mid-life desert is permeated with the dreadful
and redeeming experience of limits. Sometimes we
see only darkness. We see nothing. We hear nothing.
We feel nothing. We wonder what is happening to
our recently clear and ordered life. Then almost everything seemed to be working out. Now, we feel so
different: Will anything work out?—and, so what if it
does?

Initially, we experience the limits of our physical
selves. It is so easy to be out of physical shape at this
age. We may also feel helpless in getting back into
shape. Many of us have more ailments than we have
previously had. We are likely to become more aware
of harmful practices that affect our physical welfare.
We may begin to implement programs to improve
ourselves. We may quit smoking and drinking, or
begin dieting and exercising. In general we are more
careful in regard to our physical health.

Furthermore, often we first become aware of our
psychospiritual changes by their physical manifestation. Fatigue, weakness, tension, and depression are
indications that something has happened and is happening. Our experiences speak to us, and we should
listen to them. Weariness may mean that we have
been overactive. Tension and anxiety may be telling
us that we are overextended and fragmented. De-

pression may be saying that we have lost our dignity in our frenetic pursuit to "make it." The limits of our physical selves may be telling us to seek more than the limited.

In mid-life we are likely to have more psychological knowledge and better coping mechanisms. At the same time we experience the limits of how we cope and succeed. We become disillusioned with the popular assumption that happiness is a function of success and psychological well-being. Though we may have learned to function well, to think clearly, to speak effectively, and to act appropriately, we feel out of it. We feel confused about "it"—about what is missing. Feeling the limits of our past ways, we are challenged to see something more, to be open to the Spirit of life. We are called to face our foolish selves and to laugh at the noonday devil.

A particularly painful but redeeming experience is to be confronted with our deceptive and foolish selves. The mid-life desert is the place where we are unveiled, demasked, exposed. We come face-to-face with the ways we have deceived ourselves and others. It is the time when we are pressured to realize how we have not lived according to the values we have professed—how we have said one thing and have done another. And how we have convinced ourselves to believe what isn't so.

We can fool ourselves in many ways, often with sincere and good intentions. Many couples pretend to be happily married while they deny their misery. Many religious and ministers sincerely exhibit one life-style in public and quite another in private. Many of us seek spiritual meaning while giving ourselves too much to pleasure and success. Our repressed and rationalized truth demands recognition. Do we face our foolish selves and become wise, or do we prepare to die as fools?

There are many ways to respond to this crisis of self-disclosure. In some of us who feel inferior, latent psychological inferiority may become exacerbated. In seeing ourselves in terms of limits, we can lose perspective on past accomplishments and future possibilities and become hypercritical of ourselves. We become depressed because we see ourselves as powerless and empty. Some highly successful men who wield tremendous power feel overpowered and helpless with the experience of "nothing." Instead of responding to the spirit of the Unlimited, they seek escape in work, alcohol, and social power.

Others try to regress to youth when limits were really not an issue. For example, in a futile attempt to escape limits, a man has an affair with a younger woman. Not infrequently, a man begins to set conditions in his late thirties to have an affair in his early forties. Part of this normal madness is that it is much easier to have an affair with a young woman who may affirm his illusion of being young than to maintain an ongoing relationship with an older woman. Men who are intimidated by an older woman's maturity may engage a less threatening young adult while trying to find youthful identity.

Adolescent experiences can recur in mid-life. We

may, for instance, become preoccupied with physical appearance and behavior, so that we dress and try to act as if we were much younger. We may see them and use others as sex objects as a way of trying to recover a time of "carefree" youth.

Latent and unresolved adolescent problems can emerge to confuse and scare us. We often assume that adolescent experiences are gone forever. The truth is that both positive and negative experiences from the past continue to have an impact upon us. Thus, we can be startled with old or "seemingly new" feelings that are reminiscent of adolescence.

If, for instance, we never quite resolved our adolescent narcissism, or anger, or fragmented sexual stance, we may find ourselves in mid-life confronted again with these issues. Trying to escape the inevitable crises of limits, we might try to deceive ourselves into thinking that everything is possible and attainable—the adolescent dream of perfection. In the mid-life desert, we are called finally to give up the ways of a child and take on those of an adult.

If we fail to cope with the desert of mid-life, we will lose a great opportunity to grow spiritually. That failure may result in psychosomatic illness as well as more debilitating depression and anxiety. For example, high blood pressure, ulcers, headaches, or other such afflictions may be the result of impeded spiritual growth.

The healthy and holy response to the mid-life crisis is to leap in faith to the Unlimited. By facing our self-deception and accepting our limits, we begin to affirm our ultimate dependence on God. Consequently we transcend our helplessness. Our experience of ourselves, others, and life itself as limited, leaves us in a vacuum that draws us to the Unlimited. In nothingness, we seek Being, and paradoxically find Being in Nothingness. In our experience of Absence, we discover Presence. Instead of depending exclusively on the limited (service, possessions, or even other human beings), we surrender to the Unlimited. Depending ultimately on nothing but God, we tap an unlimited source of power.

Another confrontation with life's limits involves a new experience of time. We have the uncomfortable feeling that time is running out and not much may be left. The common phrase "time flies" becomes personally threatening when we clearly hear the loud tick of the clock winding down. We feel vulnerable to time and feel there is nothing much we can do to slow it down. Especially if time is only seen chronologically, it seems to be dreadfully beyond our control. We ask: What is time? How does time affect me? Where has time gone? What have I done with time? How much time is there? What am I going to do with the time I have left? What will happen in time? When will I die? How will I live?

To recognize that everything takes time pressures us to reevaluate our investment of time. Wherever we go and whatever we do takes time; to do one thing takes time away from other possible experiences. The experience of the limits of time throws us back on ourselves to question where and how time can be experienced best, and ultimately what we will do with the rest of our lives. The challenge is to have better times than ever before—to foster and enjoy times of the Spirit.

We are called to transcend the limits of chronological clock time, to experience kairotic time in its unlimited dimensions. Rather than living primarily according to a schedule, we can orient our life primarily around spiritual time: we can be prepared to respond to gifted moments of the Spirit. We learn that spiritual experiences cannot be rationally controlled or exactly planned for, though we can set the conditions that increase the likelihood of their happening. But they happen when they happen. We must be patient and vigilant—ready to respond when the opportunity occurs.

We discover that there is a time to listen and a time to speak, a time to fast and a time to feast, a time to mourn and a time to rejoice, a time to walk and a time to run, a time to laugh and a time to cry, a time to see and a time to be blind, a time to journey in the desert and a time to travel in the promised land, a time to live and a time to die.

Going beyond our rational control, spiritual experiences are gifts that we make time to respond to. When we totally and tightly schedule life, we have no time for the paramount experiences. We miss the permanent and recurrent kairotic times of play, wonder, love, celebration, contemplation, and joy. We must say no to important but secondary opportunities; otherwise we become overextended and too busy for more important moments. We must respond to the limits and restructure our lives in ways that invite God's presence.

In mid-life we are pressured to go beyond the immediate to the "more than," precisely while experiencing the apparent absence of Spirit. In our emptiness we desire to be fulfilled; in our sense of being lost we want to find our way. We can experience in our limits an arid absence that calls for a refreshing presence. For some of us, our ground is shaken and perhaps undermined, leaving us scared and wounded. When we gently embrace our broken selves we begin to heal and feel more a living member of the community of humankind. When we face our sinful selves we can be saved. Knowing we are broken, we can ask to be healed. Our request is always answered in time.

Spirituality becomes even more of an issue in mid-life than in previous times. The call to the interior life is greater and clearer, but unfortunately it can be misinterpreted. We can reject the beckoning of the Spirit, numb the pain of self-emergence, or simply obscure the good news. To become a full-blown workaholic, to regress, to overeat and overdrink, to repress our spirit—these and other modes of normal madness violate spiritual growth. We become fools— persons who deceive themselves and miss the ultimate and redemptive meaning of life.

We can strive to make the finite infinite. In day-to-day living we can look for more than the conventional, and eventually see more than the ordinary.

We can experience what each of us presupposes, that which radically binds us together—the Unlimited Source of Love. Fostering a contemplative disposition, we can see ourselves as various threads in the same tapestry. To appreciate that all of us are brothers and sisters is not only theoretical; it is also experiential. We can concretely see Being in beings, the Sacred in the profane, the Unlimited in the limited. Seeing so much, we take a humble stance; we come down to earth in our appreciation of life and celebrate being with one another in the Holy.

But in the desert we can feel as though we are in a barren land with no one around but ourselves. Will this be a time to come closer to or be alienated from others? Can the desert of loneliness lead to a land of love? Do we respond to the calls of others, or do we withdraw? Can we move from alienation to compassion, or do we seek to escape from community? Does resentment emerge, grow, and devour us, or does unconditional acceptance of self and others emerge? Can we learn concretely the meaning of the paschal mystery—the redemptive good of suffering in love for others?

We can also feel boxed in by our personal and professional commitments, feeling subjugated to and overstructured by them. Rather than giving life, our commitments seem to impede life. Should we continue to live for the next ten or twenty years the way we have been, or should we change? If so, how? We know that change in personal and especially in professional commitments is difficult at mid-life. Yet if

we have been deceiving ourselves, our limits call for
change. If our personal commitment has been based
only on convenience or on mere functionality, our
relationships have seriously dissipated by now and
our spirit cries out for "more than" has been. We
must admit to our charades of commitment, of pre-
tending to grow together in love. Then we can come
to reconciliation, make creative restitution, and restructure our lives for the better.

Another redemptive experience is to allow repressed feelings to emerge. For example, a married
couple who have repressed anger and resentment
for fifteen or more years can suddenly see their marriage as totally negative. They see in each other no
positive value and each resents any happiness the
other shows. Their mutual deceit was often with
good intention, for they were afraid to share their
hurt and anger. Instead, they treated each other de-
cently but did not grow much in passionate love.
Now, the price of their collusion is thrust upon them.
It is hoped that they do not separate as another way
of running from themselves. They will fare far better
to face their crisis and grow from it.

Men and women often experience mid-life differently. Many men desire to retrieve their lost youth
and fear being older. Sexist pressure moves men to
identify maturity with physical virility. Consequently many men at forty manifest a "new life" that
resembles the vigor of youth. Jogging, partying,
travel, and generally new recreational behavior
emerge. Although a woman certainly knows she is

growing older, she is more likely to respond to her limits more maturely. A woman may be freer from environmental responsibilities, thus freer for enjoying life. While women suffer as much as men, though often in different ways, many women have learned to bear their pain better than men and enjoy life more authentically.

Furthermore, many women get a second wind which enables them to cope with and even to transcend physical and sexist limits. Especially women who have dealt authentically with their early adult crisis are likely to cope well at this time. They often feel determined to improve and to explore, relying on their inner resources more than on external activities. Men, or women, who have aborted their previous adult crisis, are tempted to regress from their mid-life crisis.

At mid-life the limits of intimacy are acutely felt. A common and dangerous reaction is to expect others—parents, spouse, friends, relatives, community —to be the primary source of love. Such a reaction is understandable but futile. To depend ultimately on others for love is asking for too much, for only God is the unlimited source of love. To transcend our limits—to be loved without restriction—we must surrender primarily to God. God, and no one else, is our saving grace. Only God redeems us, not community, friends, parents, or spouse.

When we expect others to be our primary sustenance, we treat them as gods. We put them on pedestals and bind them to us as perfect ideals. Soon they

will resent our adulation, for they will be unable to
accept and learn from their limits. They will feel
powerless in being forced to be perfect, and consequently they will rebel.

Intimacy is ultimately rooted in the Spirit. Being
grounded in the primary Source of Life motivates us
to strive to love unconditionally, to manifest God.
Rooted in God's inexhaustible love, we have courage
to risk in love and the strength to accept rejection—
the ultimate test of love. Our divine dependency
enables us to love and to be loved—the basis of both
community and intimacy.

Often we feel urged to be more affectionate, but
many of us know that to love is to be vulnerable and
consequently we withdraw. Many men simply do not
know how to be authentically affectionate. Women
are usually more open to and comfortable with affection. Since relatively few men are as equally mature,
many women are left alone in the heterosocial realm.
Feeling frustration, some women may be tempted to
escape the pain. Though such a reaction is understandable, our ultimate saving grace is not a man, for
only God can save us.

In mid-life, death comes out of the shadows and
manifests itself. Rather than whispering its message,
death speaks clearly and loudly. Rather than knock-
ing at our door, death opens our door and greets us.
Death demands to be heard: Can you transcend your
culture that denies death? Can you really face and
listen to me? Can you admit your ultimate helpless-

ness? Can you transcend me—the ultimate limit? Can you live forever?

Alone with confronting our own dying, the death of grandparents and perhaps parents is also likely to occur at this time. The death and impending death of others throws us back on ourselves, asking us to reevaluate life. Accepting our own being-toward-death and recognizing our helplessness to do anything about it can lead us to transcend death, to surrender to the ultimate Unlimited that conquers the ultimate limit. Paradoxically, to accept our radical helplessness as it is clearly manifested in death leads to infinite power.

In the mid-life desert, we are tempted to demonize ourselves. In focusing too much on limits, we can lose perspective and try to escape into normally mad modes of fulfillment, such as workism, regression, drugs, or other forms of self-deception. Our mad reactions are often based on the assumption that happiness excludes limits and pain, that life should be perfect and perpetual pleasure. We may not get helpful understanding and support because many people assume that mid-lifers should know how to cope with life. We are abandoned in the desert by others, with little or no compassionate counsel. Consequently we can easily feel helpless in knowing what to do and guilty and inadequate for having such feelings.

Pragmatic efforts to purge and treat our limits rather than accept them and go beyond them also impede our growth. To be limited, to feel pain, to be in darkness are frowned upon. We feel we must "do" something to silence our spiritual questions. We can find it very difficult to respond to the challenge of mid-life, to transcend to the Unlimited.

We should seek support and help if we need it, and all of us need it. We need help to listen to the call of the desert. To share with a spouse, friend, mentor, or director, or to read spiritual books on growth, and to structure life to promote growth are all beneficial. Staying in shape physically, psychologically, and spiritually also engenders a healthy perspective. Neither to identify with limits nor to demonize ourselves, but rather to accept our limits and foster our original dependency on God are paramount.

Mid-life can be a movement deeper into hell or into heaven. It can be an exercise in frantic futility or growth in enthusiastic living. It can be a time to face our foolish selves and to become our whole selves, or it can be a time to dissipate physically, to be burdened psychologically, and to forget the spiritual life. In either case, healthy or mad, the transition passes and implementation begins.

LAND OF UNLIMITEDNESS

In our forties, we usually experience relatively less stress and lower expectations from self and others. Some of us learn to accept our limits which serve as a springboard to the Unlimited, or we try to deny them, or escape from them and become more severely limited. Some of us have faced our demonic selves while others continue to run from the dark side of life. Rejecting and running from the mid-life desert leads to an impotent life. Accepting and learning in the desert brings us closer to the Promised Land of Unlimited Power.

When we depend on God, life becomes progressively transcendent and we go beyond our limits. Having entered the shadow of ourselves, we emerge enlightened and renewed. Instead of unconsciously demanding heaven, we celebrate being on earth— the prelude to the Kingdom. We live with more joy and spirit. When we accept life's limits, love grows. We become compassionate persons who help and heal. We realize that the commitment to love compassionately is essential precisely because we are limited. Such an open and steadfast love gives us direction and solidarity in living a life that ultimately makes sense.

In experiencing the limits of love, we accept them and foster an unconditional love. However, if we have built up anger and hurt from the past, we are likely to express resentment at this time. Rather than accepting our resentment and understanding it, we repress love. We see others only in terms of their limits instead of embracing their limits in love. Rather than helping them, we retaliate with hostility and fail to grow in love. It is hoped that we will not lose love by taking it for granted or settle for counterfeits of love. Love will be our saving sustenance.

We can go through the motions of living when we

live without love. We can structure our lives in unauthentic ways, often because we have not truly confronted ourselves. In not accepting our limits, we
may try to become unlimited with hyperactivity, or
numb the pain of being mortal through drugs.
Though we feel superficially alive, we always come
back to ourselves—beings-toward-death. Running
from life, we feel tired, beat, and less alive. Simply to
exist becomes a heavy effort.

Opting for the Spirit, however, we become more
spirited and alive. Our limits affirm that we are ultimately unlimited. In spite of our lost youth, we become more beautiful—persons who integrate their
physical, psychological, and spiritual dimensions. We
accept and understand the stress of a life that leads
to death, and rather than depending only on social
sciences to save us, we also rely on God.

As mid-lifers we are likely to have more bills and
responsibilities than before, but also more opportunities and more money. How we use money and social
power is highly dependent on our spiritual status.
Running from spirituality increases the likelihood
that we will measure the meaning of life by what we
have rather than by who we are. We can continue to
fool ourselves.

It is imperative that we nourish our spiritual lives.
It is easy to take growth for granted in relatively
settled times, particularly in a culture that does not
actively promote and reward spirituality. It is good to
reflect on our recent critical past and to live with a
sense of the Unlimited. We should foster a "contem-

plative disposition"—"seeing" more than is apparent. Experiencing the Unlimited in the midst of daily limits enables us to dance with life. We celebrate the mystery of living, laugh at life, and keep a divine perspective. We become enthusiastic persons.

As in crisis, however, we can displace our yearning for the spiritual with activities that satisfy temporarily. Rather than responding authentically to the call of the Spirit, we become displaced persons—fragmented, hollow, shallow, and lost. We lose our original Spirit, the love that binds us in community. Without a spiritual vision, we play games or become withdrawn and settle for less than is possible. We live without authentic community, without being together in God's love.

Sexuality should become better in mid-life. We can become true men and women—integral persons who feel freer to incorporate the attributes of the other sex. Men, for instance, can become more affectionate and women more assertive. Both sexes can feel freer to nourish, assert, give, and receive. We can become authentically androgenous.

The affective dimension of sexuality can also be better integrated and appreciated. We realize that we can touch not only genitally but also affectively, that we can be intimate without genital relations. Men particularly can more fully realize the possibilities of affective sexuality as a beautiful end in itself. Integrated with spirituality, genitality has more depth, flexibility, and fulfillment. Its consequences linger longer and significantly influence our everyday life. Thus men in particular need not be impotent or less sexual but rather more sexually fulfilled.

When we embrace the Spirit within us, everything in life improves, including play. Vacations are not simply a time to recuperate from work, but are chronological opportunities to renew and engender kairotic times. The aesthetic dimension of nature and art also becomes vibrantly real, enlightening everyday living. We can appreciate Being in anything, particularly in what we are apt to take for granted. The common ground on which all people stand is seen as the Spirit we manifest. Art and architecture, creating and challenging, things used and enjoyed, show the glory of the Presence.

Living spiritually helps us to become more creative, flexible, and productive workers. Our ministry is grounded in, sustained by, and a manifestation of our love. Without growing in love, we become disenchanted. Work has little meaning, or we become workaholics who make work our god. To be sure, we can succeed in work, but functional success is not our ultimate value. Though work is very important, it is at best secondary to "useless" love. Actually, the most significant form of ministry is to be uselessly present in love. To affirm and touch in love are more important than to give functional service.

Mid-life is the critical time to realize that death and dying can help us live more fully. We are more able to help those who mourn the death of loved ones as well as comfort ourselves in death. We realize that in certain ways dead people are more alive in their disembodiment, more present in their absence than in their physical presence. Though we miss them, our loved ones stay alive forever.

We should continue to slow down to see the Unlimited in the limited. Changing pace, seeing new landscapes, or old landscapes in new ways, and taking a contemplative posture in everyday living can be critical to continued growth. Take time for kairotic events. Truly to feast on feast days and to celebrate on holy days are ways to remind ourselves of the Unlimited in everyday living. Paradoxically, in the limits of embodiment we are invited to dance with the Unlimited. It is the Time.

6

MIDDLE-AGED ADULTHOOD

APPROACHING FIFTY, we make the transition from the mid-life years to middle age. Far removed from youth and approaching the elderly years, we are closer to death than to birth, yet by grace, we may live another quarter century or more. There is no doubt, however, that we are closing in on the destiny of life—death.

Like other transitional phases, middle age evokes new role expectations from self and others. Young people treat us differently, and we might feel that we are over the hump and on a descending path. Actually coming to middle age can be devastating for those who escaped from the mid-life crisis, for rather than transcending limits, they can become depressed and strangled by them.

Tired of being challenged, we might refuse to enter the desert of middle age. Common physical changes such as circulatory problems, weight gain, loss or graying of hair, and joint problems can make entering the desert ominous. We can regard it with foreboding, or we can anticipate it as a challenge. If we have grown through our previous crises, we are likely to take this one as another opportunity for growth.

DESERT OF DEPRESSION

The middle-aged desert can be painful or insightful. Previous desert journeys have made experiences like depression and death familiar rather than foreign and fatal. Psychologically we cope with and learn from these dark nights, and spiritually we become more intimate with the source of our being: Our Father.

Depression in middle age is common. It may be rooted in environmental changes. For example, if we have centered our life exclusively around our family, we may indeed be depressed when our family leaves. A woman who derives her personal satisfaction from mothering will experience significant loss and consequent depression when her children leave home. Or middle-aged couples whose marriage has been one of adjustment rather than of healthy love have reason to be depressed. Some persons with no history of mental illness undergo involutional melancholia, a psychotic disorder characterized by severe depression, anxiety, insomnia, and frequent guilt and somatic preoccupation. Such an illness can immobilize one and bring one to the brink of despair.

Besides these forms of depression, spiritual depression also emerges. Rather than being depressed for psychological and perhaps physical reasons, we are depressed about nothing in particular. We feel at a loss to say what is going on except that nothing much makes sense. Even though we may have lived a meaningful and worthwhile life, now at times we feel that our reason for being has deserted us.

Such depression is an opportunity to slow down, to reflect, and to re-collect life. In depression, we can listen to the reality that invites us to embrace our radical poverty—a nothingness that affirms our ultimate helplessness and calls for dependency on God. Going beyond all things, or experiencing nothing, we come closer to the ground out of which all beings emerge and are kept alive. Out of our depression we become more enthusiastic and fulfilled.

At middle age, feelings of guilt and failure are quite common. We can feel guilty about acts committed twenty or thirty years ago, or we can feel a sense of failure for some long since missing opportunities. If we are inclined to be compulsive, we may blame ourselves for not perfectly realizing all our aims and objectives. Anything less than perfection appears to be a source of guilt and feeling of failure. Life appears irreversible and certain opportunities missed are irrevocably gone. When referring to the future, we feel that life is shorter than it really is; consequently we feel helpless to change things. Besides, we feel exhausted from trying to do the impossible—control life.

Anger and resentment are not uncommon at this time. A persistent feeling of indignant disapproval may be due to anger that has built up over years, perhaps due to hurt or neglect by parents or superiors. Middle-agers who over many years submitted to mistreatment may not blatantly express their pent-up feelings. Instead of taking everything, they now take nothing. Such resentment is often our human and futile attempt to affirm our dignity. No longer are we going to be used as doormats; now we start walking on other people. At least we will no longer be lowered and used. We demand recognition.

In a similar way, middle-agers who have been dependent most of their lives may suddenly become independent. Rather than always saying yes, they now say no to almost everything. Whatever the case, destructive behavior should not be condoned, but angry feelings can be accepted and channeled in service of freedom. Always look at what such angry feelings and behaviors mean, for often they are overreactions or overcompensations for past dependency.

Some middle-agers feel that life has gone "down the drain," and they blame others for mistreating them. Indeed, their anger and resentment often indicate an uncomfortable truth: many middle-agers have been mistreated. They were used as mere functionaries rather than respected as persons of worth. These abused middle-agers should be aware of what has happened, but take responsibility to change their lives without being vindictive. The "exploiters" should admit their guilt and foster attitudes and actions that affirm the dignity of persons.

In middle age we may become irritated with

young people. It bothers us to see how youth is spoiled in being given so much while expecting so little. Many middle-agers struggled intensely to get an education, while younger people with open opportunities do not take advantage of them. Or we get irritated when younger people get vacations and other recreational opportunities which we never got and still do not get.

Many people assume that middle-agers understand their feelings, and by virtue of their age know how to cope with life's pressures. Being middle-aged is no guarantee of understanding affective living. Though we may be good functionaries, we can be relatively ignorant of feelings and affective relationships. To demand what middle-agers cannot give can be totally unfair. We should take a more careful look at the inner lives of middle-agers. Behind the mask of functional competency we might find sensitive persons who are psychosocially and spiritually naive, and too ignorant and scared to find ways to nourish themselves.

Modern middle-agers find it difficult to make positive sense out of apparently negative feelings. They were raised in a period that minimized or even repressed affective expression. Sharing affectively, close friendships, and personal openness were not only minimized, they were often punished. The focus was on behavior often at the expense of inner feelings and experience. To do what was expected was reinforced, while affective expression and intimacy were simply ignored or punished. Thus, rather than learning to express or act on their feelings, they learned to restrict and often repress them. For example, they were taught to feel guilty about anger, and not to act on it. To accept anger and benefit from it was seldom a possibility; rather, anger brought the promise of rejection from self or others. Such middle-agers need appreciation and help.

Middle age brings a crisis of reconciliation. Our challenge is to reflect on life and say yes rather than no to it. We need to come to a sense of integrity with self, others, and the world. Out of depression we come to a sense of fulfillment. Out of guilt we come to forgive ourselves and others. Out of limits we come to a deeper sense of the unlimited. Out of resentment we affirm our dignity and learn to be compassionate and forgiving. Out of anger we become gentle. This is the age of atonement—to become one with ourselves and others. The time is for joy.

In middle age we experience a contest of integrity versus worthlessness. Questions emerge. Can I become a whole rather than a fragmented person? Can I integrate my physical and social and my spiritual selves rather than focus too much on one or two at the expense of others? Do I repress my spirit? Can every day be a source of emergent meaning rather than another day to get through?

If we reject our feelings, we can become depressed about being depressed. Feeling stuck in a dark pit, we fixate on our faults, limits, emptiness, and relatively short future. Too easily we flee from these desert opportunities. We can even despair, feeling that

life is absurd. If earlier we have run from life's radical
questions, we are likely to pay our debt at this time.
Still, some of us escape. But even though we succeed
in silencing the Spirit, we become displaced and fragmented. The Hound of Heaven will not give up on
us. He will catch us in our elderly years, or surely in
death.

Consider how physical changes can affect a man's
spiritual life. Usually in the early fifties, men experience a decline in strength, endurance, and sexual
desire. There is also a subtle decline in so-called masculine qualities—one may develop a higher-pitched
voice, less facial hair, and wider hips. Some men feel
anxious about pressure to perform sexually. Generally men suffer discomfort from depression, insomnia, digestive disturbances, nervousness, and fatigue,
tingling sensations in extremities, irritability, aches
and pains. Many men manifest personality changes
in reaction to these physical changes.

The female climacteric changes are usually more
overt and acute than a man's. Menopause usually
occurs around this time. The cessation of menstruat-
ing along with other bodily and emotional changes
can compound the stress women feel during this
time of transition.

Hormonal changes bring a generalized atrophy of
the reproductive system. The lack of estrogen and
progesterone perhaps accounts for some decline in
so-called feminine appearance. Secondary sex char-
acteristics become less pronounced. Facial hair may
become coarser, the voice may deepen, body curves

may flatten out, and breasts may appear flabby. Furthermore, discomfort such as hot flashes, sweating, flushes, bodily tingling, headaches, fatigue, and nervousness are not rare. Possible weight gain, which is centered around the abdomen and hips, may make a woman look heavier than she is. What all this means to a woman is highly contingent on cultural and environmental attitudes, as well as her own views.

Middle-agers who place too much value on how they look are likely to experience considerable stress, which may be manifested in cardiovascular and gastrointestinal disorders. If we have been physically and functionally hyperactive while repressing our spiritual life, we may find ourselves unable to cope with such changes.

Ideally, physical changes can be transcended. The challenge is to see more than loss. When we focus on loss we are likely to become depressed in a negative, unproductive way. There are positive opportunities for growth. For instance, rather than leading to loss of self-esteem, menopausal changes can engender freedom from pregnancy and menstruation that can help some women enjoy sex and life more than ever. Middle-aged women, however, continue to intimidate many men. Perhaps that may be a reason why men consider them no longer attractive or as "neuter" in spite of contradictory evidence. Such sexual oppression is man's way of hiding from his own insecurity and impotence.

Considerable psychological and social stress is common to middle age. For instance, it is the time of the so-called empty nest. A woman (or a man) who has centered life around her children is thrown into a crisis when the children leave. No longer can she invest her time, energy, and love in her children. Now she feels lost. Actually a woman has good reason to feel depressed about such a state of affairs, but her challenge is to renew herself.

Often men cannot even listen as women express their feelings. Such men, incapable of sharing, run from their crisis. A relatively common way to escape is to turn to alcohol. Alcoholism is a major problem for men between the ages of forty-five and sixty-four. It can be an attempt to numb the feelings of depression, emptiness, loneliness, and personal failure.

A successful resolution to the middle-aged crisis leads to an easier resolution in the elderly years. In fact, women adjust better than men to the elderly years because women work through their middle-aged crisis better than men. They learn to be more independent, they are stronger, and can endure more than men as they grow older. Adjusting to environmental changes and facing the pain of self-renewal, women build a strong foundation for the second half of their adult lives.

Sexuality is a particularly critical area in the middle-aged crisis. How we resolve our crisis highly determines our future sexual life. Fundamental questions are asked. Am I still a man? Am I still a woman? Have I been an authentic male or female person? Will I continue to be one? Too many men and women feel insecure about their primary sexuality and consequently doubt themselves. If we have focused too much on physical attraction and functional performance, we can have a painful crisis. Men who emphasize genital sex at the expense of affective and primary sexuality can be in dire difficulty. These men may continue to practice sad charades of youth in trying to become Don Juans. For others, however, middle age is an excellent time to deepen the efforts already started in mid-life—to become more integral sexual persons.

Genital sex comes to a clear crisis. Researchers indicate that people who withdraw from genital sex find it increasingly more difficult to reenter it. Studies such as those of Masters and Johnson show that sexual inadequacy increases sharply after age fifty for men. The prognosis is poor for those who assume that they are "too old" for such things and who have not consistently practiced loving sex.

Other changes also occur. Friends, peers, and parents are nearing death or have died. We go to the weddings of our children and of the children of relatives and friends. Since we feel older and are becoming the senior family members, we take more responsibility in family and community affairs. We become the leaders. We take the place of our parents.

Actually, parent-child roles may reverse somewhat. Sometimes, especially if we have not had much contact with our parents, we may know them for the first time outside their parental roles. This can cause difficulties for both parents and middle-aged children. Old suppressed problems may emerge and cause hurt and resentment. Or on the other hand, we and our parents can become companions and learn to enjoy each other more than ever.

However, in the lonely trails of the middle-aged desert we can feel lost, unloved, and unworthy of love. Even though loved ones tell us that they love us, we can feel deserted and doubt them. Though we cognitively know that others love us, we feel alone and uncomfortably empty. Too often friends and family, with good intentions, encourage us to be our old selves instead of inviting us to become new selves. Those who love us with real love will embrace us no matter what, including our doubts and changes of behavior. The intent is not to condone or reinforce negative behavior but to love unconditionally. Loneliness and self-doubt should deepen and strengthen love by helping us become more aware of ourselves, more compassionate for others, and more dependent on God.

A middle-aged spiritual challenge is to foster a transcendent love that goes beyond the vicissitudes of living to the common ground of all experience. Love helps us to transcend our differences in realizing that all of us are parts of the same body. We see in love the mystery that underlies and goes infinitely beyond our problems. Responding in the midst of brokenness, we become wounded and compassionate healers. Even in the absence of interpersonal intimacy, we hunger for the intimacy that always nourishes. Starving for more than what we can give ourselves, we admit our radical poverty—that we cannot earn our spiritual food. We can only ask for the gift of salvation.

We again affirm and deepen our radical dependency on the Source of our powers. We reaffirm that we are helpless in making permanent sense of our human condition, that on our own we can ultimately do little. We give up trying to control our destiny. Rather than futilely trying to save ourselves, we surrender to God. Then, our emptiness is fulfilled; our helplessness engenders power; our poverty brings riches; our loneliness evokes love.

If we have derived too much of our worth from work, we are likely to undergo a painful reevaluation. Feeling physically tired, psychologically drained, socially disenchanted, we can experience a spiritual crisis of work. Some of us continue to be workaholics and become tense, exhausted, and depressed. Others who feel burnt out become helplessly afraid of renewing life, or they simply do not know how and feel guilty.

Paradoxically, our relative lack of vitality can lead to new vitality. We challenge ourselves to recreate so that play with self and others is renewed. Play is especially useful in fostering a gentle and spirited mode of being. Having more time and different energy, we manifest more consistently a playful spirit. In playing with Spirit, we celebrate everyday living.

There are many middle-agers, however, who simply do not know how to play. A background of workism and affective repression makes it difficult to foster a playful spirit. A few seek to become playboys or playgirls to numb the pain of self-renewal. Others become too passive, letting life pass them by. Some increase their socializing but only in service of work —becoming too busy to live authentically. Many middle-agers have to learn to play without guilt. Many have to be taught to restructure their lives to guarantee time and space to learn to enjoy being useless.

As we grow older, death and dying become clearly critical. If we have run from death, it usually catches us at this time. Though some of us can still escape the grasp of death, we will eventually be caught in our elderly years. The main issue in escaping death is that we consequently miss much of life.

If we have denied death most of our lives, death now demands to be recognized. Our dreadful response can be our saving grace. No longer does death whisper, silently open our door, or walk in our room; death comes up to us, shakes our hand, and speaks loudly and clearly. Death looks at us, touches us, and talks to us. Death holds us and asks us how we have been living, what we have been doing with the last quarter of our lives. Death pleads with us to live.

A recurrent obstacle is to "double-feel"—to feel negatively about a feeling. For instance, we can feel depressed or guilty about feeling depressed and guilty. Though normal, such a coping mechanism is not healthy, for it only makes pain and tension worse. Alcoholism as well as obsession with work and social activities, is an obstacle that blocks healthy self-emergence. Since our feelings are intense and deep, we can be pressured to numb them, or use mad coping mechanisms that can be carried over into the remaining years. In this case we continue to fight ourselves and become increasingly miserable.

Too often, well-intentioned persons try to help middle-agers in negative ways; they offer help that hinders. Family, friends, and professionals may pressure middle-agers to be their "old selves," making them feel guilty for going through what they experience. Such help assumes that feelings of depression and guilt are necessarily unhealthy. Rather than giving psychological space and time, such counsel actually aborts growth. It behooves middle-agers to beware of well-intentioned but negative help.

A particular danger of the middle-age crisis is to conform to cultural and personal expectations. For instance, it is not uncommon for women to fulfill the sexist prophecy that menopause means the end of being a true woman and of an enjoyable sex life. Besides lowering their self-esteem which can engender depression, women who follow such a false script can become unattractive and insipid, just the opposite of what they can be. Men can also be sexist victims by falsely assuming that middle age means a restricted rather than an expanding life. Rather than being a depressed life, the desert of middle age is the way to a more spirited, joyful life.

LAND OF JOY

Middle age can be a joyful time to harvest the fruits of desert planting, or it can be a barren land with little hope. Since middle age can last fifteen or more years, it offers a long time of misery or joy.

Middle age is our last time of being "not old." Although these years are times of settling down rather than restructuring life, the fifties include preparing for the elderly years, especially those of retirement. Learning new avocations and deepening old ones can be helpful. Paramount, however, is living a spiritual life, without which all activities quickly become boring.

Life implies death and death incorporates life. One without the other is an illusion. Death becomes a life-force that motivates integral and spiritual living. Paradoxically, a deeper awareness and appreciation of death enables us to enjoy life more than ever. We come alive when we transcend death by touching eternal life.

Death of loved ones, which is likely to occur at this time, radically changes our lives. When a beloved one dies, our present experience, past memories, and future possibilities change significantly. Such a death creates experiential gaps that disrupt familiar relationships and upsets our community. Death also makes us more aware of the value of life and encourages us to live fully. But death and the little deaths of depression, loneliness, and guilt are often painfully misunderstood. They are rejected, and their inducement to grow in holiness and healthiness are closed off.

The death of persons significant to us, family changes such as our children leaving home, our children marrying, and career success or failure bring back memories. We reflect on two or three decades that have passed. A married couple may look at their married sons and daughters and feel that it was only yesterday that they were children. They may even see themselves as grandparents more than as parents. And yet we might not feel as old as we are. Where has the time gone? Middle-aged milestones incorporate a history that makes for fulfillment or emptiness.

Instead of futilely trying to escape from limits, we accept and transcend them. Although we may not eat as much, we can enjoy each meal as a small feast. Sleeping habits may change, but we can enjoy sleep rather than seeing it only as a way to recuperate. Activity is valued more by its quality than by its quantity. In this way, we come to a new physical vigor. We become adept at self-expression that manifests a gentle and graceful touch. Even if physical sickness comes, which now is more likely, we can transcend it, at least by not identifying with it. We truly become an embodiment of Spirit.

It is wise to keep ourselves in good physical, psychosocial, and spiritual condition. To keep our activity level consistent rather than sporadic, and to maintain a nutritious, low-calorie diet can be important.

There is a temptation to succumb to ageism in middle age, to become flabby, flat, and sedentary. Physical care and exercise can build the infrastructure that makes us more available for play, sexuality, and spirited living.

To slow down and to see life in its sacred dimensions can bring a wealth of fulfillment rather than emptiness. Paradoxically, such active slowing down can bring on inner activity that evokes more fulfillment and satisfaction than external hyperactivity. An obstacle, however, is that many middle-agers do not know how to slow down, to enjoy, to take vacations, to see things differently, to do nothing. Many may be embarrassed to ask for help. Invite them to broaden their recreative landscapes. Gently and persistently pressure them to explore new lands. To experience spirituality in everyday living and to observe special occasions such as feast days and holy days are also important.

In middle age we can have a good measure of common sense so that our judgments are prudent rather than compulsive or impulsive. We are unlikely to be lured down blind alleys and more likely to cope well. By this time, most of us have learned some techniques that help to lessen the wear and tear of normal living. We have learned how to reduce the internal and external sources of debilitating stress.

We also find new interests or renew old ones. We take the time to enjoy activities, arts, reading, and people. Becoming grandparents may enable us to renew playful times or compensate for missed opportunities with our own children. Knowing now from experience what pleases and fulfills, we might take self-improvement courses. Actually, increasing numbers of middle-agers are returning to school in one form or another.

Middle age can be a particularly good time to deepen and enjoy our community. Besides becoming members of a powerful political and economic generation, we can come into closer communion with humankind. Above all, we deepen our community ties by celebrating its binding force—the Spirit of God. Rather than growing in resentment and bitterness over past injustices and failures, we can grow and enjoy communal living. Married people now have more time to be with each other sexually, socially, and spiritually. Their spousal union of head and heart, their sharing and fostering of mutual values, and their spiritual oneness increase. While respecting each other's need for solitude and individuality, they come closer to being one.

Middle age can also be the time to reap the fruits of our interpersonal labor. We can take delight in knowing that we have influenced our children to become responsible adults. We can begin to see how our interpersonal struggles and sacrifices have led to solid relationships. We can experience joy and satisfaction in being veteran members of a community.

Genital sex may be less frequent; it can be qualitatively better. As middle-agers we are more aware of ourselves and can be fuller men and women. We can celebrate being with each other. We can communicate on a deeper level so that our communication fosters communion. Men can be more gentle and affectionate and women can freely proclaim themselves. Seeing through sexist games and prejudices, we appreciate and enjoy each other. Fewer sex differences are apparent in activities, interests, and interpersonal relationships. As men and women, we come closer to being one of a kind.

Spiritual meaning can now be experienced everywhere, in everyone, and in everything. Seeing with spiritual eyes enables us to enjoy an inexhaustible source of fulfilling meaning. Paradoxically, we experience "more" than we experience. We realize that there is more to life than what happens to us. We live with a perpetual sense of surprise, with a sense that each day, each hour, each moment, something full of wonder may happen. Kairotic times become more frequent and evident.

Such contemplative living is active. It is not magical musing, sentimental self-deception, or spiritual nonsense. It is concrete, practical, and fulfilling. It is a different way of seeing, a way that transcends time and space.

We see the spiritual where it is hidden. We know that people who are living normally mad lives by exploiting and manipulating others are actually running away from happiness. We appeal to the Spirit in them. Rather than trying to convince them of the Spirit, we respond to their spirit in their apparent nonsense. This contemplative view pierces through the facades of evil and madness to the underlying goodness.

Middle age is the time when compassion is truly broadened and deepened. We help one another bear the weight of existence. Rather than becoming alienated from others and falling into loveless loneliness, we strive to embrace everyone in love. Instead of preparing for a life of loneliness or hyperdependency, our loneliness promotes dependency on God —our perpetual source of love.

Middle age is the time when transcendence is deepened qualitatively and quantitatively. We experience the underlying ground of all realities, so that our lives are meaningful no matter what, including times when we are physically or psychologically ill. We really celebrate everyday living, praising God's Being in all beings. Instead of living superficially and settling for much less than is possible, instead of focusing on the surface of reality, and instead of living nervously and restlessly, we concretely and compassionately transcend to a deep and sustaining source of peace.

Wisdom also becomes a central motivating force. Though wisdom is not entirely absent before middle age, it now blossoms. Seeing with the eyes of eternity, we see light in darkness and darkness in light. We transcend the information of rational knowledge to a transrational appreciation of life. Seeing with our inner eye, we appreciate more than our senses allow. Knowing by unknowing, we stand under more than is rationally possible.

Middle age should be a prime time to mature. Though formal education can be a help to some, more important is the informal education, reading, and especially a general appreciation of life. The key challenge is to grow spiritually, and consequently cope with and transcend limits, depression, and ultimately death.

Healthy middle-agers foster a playful and loving style of living—a life of celebration. Celebrations structure chronological times for engendering and remembering kairotic events that enable us to enjoy the reason and ground of our beings. To stand in awe, to give thanks and praise, to laugh and cry, to eat and drink with spirit rekindles and affirms sacred times while renewing our spirit. With Spirit, we dance.

7

ELDERLY
ADULTHOOD

A POPULAR ASSUMPTION in Western culture is that
the elderly years mark the end rather than the zenith
of life. We tend to look toward old age with controlled trepidation rather than joyful expectation. As
a result we fail to appreciate these last years of adulthood. Our aim is to present the elderly years as the
most spirited time on earth. We see the Spirit of life
most fully and integrally manifest in these years. Indeed, this season can be a time of feasting, not a time
of fasting. It can be a time for a spiritual banquet.

Perhaps because of our fears of old age, much
money and effort have been invested in the study of
being elderly (gerontology), and the treatment of elderly people (geriatrics). Studies centering around
genetic inheritance, stress management, environmental conditions such as climate, housing, social involvement, economic stability, nutrition, and medical care have increased. Educational, political, social,
and recreational organizations and programs have
also increased significantly. Such studies and pro-

101

grams are important indeed. The area that has been
most neglected, however, is the spiritual. This is un-
fortunate for any age group, but especially so for
those who are peaking spiritually. Thus, our focus,
even more than with the previous stages of development, is on the spiritual life.

A familiar sight emerges on the horizon of the elderly years—the desert. Rather than being surprised
by such a vision, seasoned travelers expect it and
make the journey, perhaps for the last time.

DESERT OF DEATH

Every life crisis is a crisis of life and death. At no
other time is death so insistent as in the elderly years.
Death firmly questions us. Is life affirmed, nourished,
and pursued? Or is life rejected and stopped? Do we
disengage not only from social activities but also from
life itself, or do we engage life more deeply? Is our
spirit manifested more strongly and clearly, or is our
spirit dying? Can we say yes to our past and affirm our
future? Or do we seek to escape from life, rationalize
its meaning, and deny its value?

No longer are we thinking about death; no longer
is death peeking through our keyhole; no longer
does death talk to us; no longer does death shake
our hand. Now, death embraces us. Is death a friend
or an enemy? Have we faced it before so that death
is almost a friend? Or have we run from death as
from an enemy? Have we tried to deny the obvi-
ous? Can we continue to say yes to an unknown fu-

ture that incorporates an impending inescapable death? Despite all evidence, do we feel that we will never die, or that death is for "them," not for us? Can we face death and foster life? Can we look at death's stare with eyes of love? Can we conquer death?

If we have listened to death in the middle years and before, it will hold no terror for us now. The desert of death, however, can look overwhelming to those who have denied death. Nothing is left except the desert, and some die in the desert long before it is necessary. Rather than reaching its zenith, life becomes meaningless and inert. But instead of leading to despair, this final desert can be our saving grace. It can be experienced as a springboard to eternal life.

The elderly years present us with our last chance to live or die. We are called to choose life or death. Though our bodies may have dissipated considerably, the desert of old age is another challenge to deepen life, to go on, to grow.

Our assumptions, however, highly influence our final journey. Those of us who assume that old age is diminution rather than culmination of life can be devastated in their elderly years. Persons who are part of a family or of a religious community, or who have close friends, are likely to fare better than those who are single or widowed. Although happiness is not primarily a reward of money, financial resources are necessary to satisfy basic needs and to open up certain opportunities. Few persons enjoy aesthetic

and spiritual living if their more basic functional
needs are not met.

It is imperative in the elderly years to rekindle, to
reaffirm, and to nourish our spiritual lives. Because
we have more time to listen to the Spirit, a danger
is to postpone our spiritual concerns. Changes in personal and social situations require adjustments. We
have to be careful that we do not adjust psychosocially at the expense of spiritual growth.

Becoming relatively disengaged, however, from
previous roles and functional responsibilities can
help us to deepen our spiritual lives. Rather than
finding activities that simply fill up time, we should
look for activities that rekindle and renew our spirit.
Such an approach is not difficult to follow if it has
been cultivated for years before retirement. Since
we are less easily seduced by the cultural madness
about us, we are freer to hear the Holy Spirit in
ourselves and others. Being somewhat detached
from conventional life enables us to see abnormally;
that is, to see more than is normally seen.

We again feel called to reflect on our commitment
to love. Acknowledging that these will be our last
years together, we are called to deepen our marital
commitment. If we are widowed, it becomes as important for us to adjust to loneliness as to economic,
medical, and social problems. If we are single, our
reference groups are important. They provide occasions for sharing values and interests, as well as giving
understanding and support. And if we are a member

of a community, we question its value as a source of appreciation and help as well as an opportunity to help and guide. If we have lived without a permanent commitment to love, we can be devastated by our impending death, or the crisis can evoke in us a permanent sense of everlasting life.

Death persistently and loudly asks how and why we are living, while life patiently awaits our answers. It raises questions about integrity. Am I whole? Am I a truthful person in touch with my whole self and with others? Have I merely lived a cerebral existence? Have I placed too much emphasis on what I have, rather than on who I am? Those who have lived a fragmented and disassociated life feel displaced—anxiously groundless, out of touch with the heart of the matter.

Along with integrity, we question our worth. Where does my worth lie? What is my worth? Am I worthwhile? Do I appreciate my own dignity? Has life been worth the struggle? Am I worthy of love, of life? Do I feel worthless? Am I an absolute nothing? Do I mean little or nothing to anyone? to myself? to God? Am I a person of dignity and integrity?

In our final years we acutely experience the need for God. Our redemption lies in becoming companions with the Person who is the Sustaining Source of our dignity and integrity, of our being. We can sit down with our Creator, converse with him, give thanks, break bread, and be healed. The desert of death is conquered with Life. No matter what illness, deprivation, loneliness, or rejection, we humbly appreciate the truth that we are people of infinite worth.

A life rooted in God's love manifests dignity and finds meaning and fulfillment in any circumstances. If we say yes to ourselves, to others, to life, then the present, past, and future make sense. However, if we have become fragmented and displaced, if we minimize our dignity, though we may be surrounded by everything we ever wanted, we come to despair. Our past charades become senseless and no longer evoke applause. Life becomes radically frustrating and ultimately terminal.

There is always hope. Even if we have never entered the desert, the crisis of the elderly years can be an invitation to discover our lost spirit. It can challenge and motivate us to accept our source of integrity, dignity, and eternal fulfillment. Even though we see little sense to life, we still have time to say yes to the present and the future, and ask to be forgiven for our past. In reconciling ourselves, we realize that our integrity and dignity are grounded in God. Rather than finding life empty, we come closer to being permanently fulfilled—to the Kingdom of God.

Past values, healthy or mad, are reexamined. We are challenged in a new way to love and suffer with and for others. Do we alienate ourselves from others and become bitter and fester in hate? Do we see everyone as "out there" rather than being part of us? Can we transcend the cultural madness of ageism and even understand it while forgiving? Can we offer our suffering as a sacrifice—an act that makes life redemptive, that heals a suffering with a compassion that engenders holiness and healthiness? Suffering for others is necessary to become whole, to lessen our alienation from the Holy. We believe that death leads to life.

In spite of our physical decline, we can become more physical than ever in that we can manifest our spirit more powerfully than ever. Centering ourselves in the Spirit, we can reject the cultural trend to overemphasize the physical and the functional. Our arthritic hands can show more spirit and beauty than our once sensual young hands. We can better touch and be touched. We can read and respond to the embodiment of others. Incarnating the Spirit, we are infinitely present and touchable.

A paradoxical phenomenon often occurs in the elderly years; though our bodies look old, are old, and in many ways feel old, we can feel "childlike." When people treat us as old and lifeless, it may be difficult to be spirited. We must proclaim our spirit and refuse to identify with a dying body; we must renew our incarnated spirit and show delight.

Many elderly people disengage from social activities. Although various senior citizens groups promote significant and enjoyable activities, many elderly are still inclined to be uninvolved. Our economic status influences our activities and interests to some degree. However, rich or poor, there is little need for us to become socially dead. In fact, our spiritual crisis can engender a new social interest.

Becoming more spiritual, we can enjoy more than ever vacations, trips, a walk, or simply celebrating the routine of living.

The inevitable fact is that the elderly years call forth the spiritual infinitely more than before. Now we are more able to transcend—to go beyond our physical, social, and psychological confinement. We can see the unity that underlies all our differences. We experience all races, ethnic groups, ages, and the sexes as parts of the same reality. But we can still be seduced by normal superficial behavior of only responding to the surface aspects of reality. Our saving grace is to respond to the call of the "more than" which is present in every aspect of life.

But some of us withdraw and grow grumpy, and people may wonder what is happening to us. A frequent reason for our nasty behavior is that we have identified life with work and minimized life's nonfunctional spiritual dimensions. Consequently we protest at having nothing to do. Rather than being recognized as we once were, we are now tolerated, criticized, or misunderstood, for it is thought that we serve no useful purpose. Too many of us leave the last day of work on Friday, enjoy Saturday and Sunday, and get up for work on Monday. Finding that we have no work, we relax. But by Monday afternoon we begin to seek things to do. After a few days when we have fixed everything twice, we search for anything to do. In due course after forcing ourselves to be active, we have to come back to ourselves. We have to realize that identifying life with work is not the Way.

Women usually adjust better than men to the relative absence of work. Women maintain their work, outside or inside the home, and those men who help around the house also have less difficulty making this vocational transition. Often it is advisable to find part-time work—one can serve as a consultant or as a volunteer in social services. Such activity brings meaning and bridges the gap between middle and elderly years.

Unfortunately, elderly people often find themselves by themselves. The death of a spouse is likely to cause a difficult adjustment to living with and by oneself. A man, for instance, has been subtly dependent on his wife in domestic matters. He can easily feel depressed, lost, and helpless without her. A woman is more likely to find herself alone than a man is. A woman is likely to marry at a younger age and live more than seven years longer than a man.

Some couples are fortunate to live together well into their elderly years. If they have lived authentically with each other, these years are their happiest. Loving couples need no words to say, "I love you." They can be purely present to each other without saying much. In a real way their concern for each other has grown from an affective feeling to contemplative love. But couples who have gone their separate ways will probably be miserable. Their efforts to adjust to their situation often leads to withdrawal from each other, leaving them alone and lonely— strangers living together.

Furthermore, elderly people often lose the authority they once had in the family and society. Instead of giving them genuine respect, we often patronize and tolerate them. We seldom go to them for advice and comfort, which is ironic because the elderly should be most qualified to console and sustain us, especially spiritually. When we minimize the spiritual, we consequently have no reason to consult them. Far from being spiritual counselors, many old people are irritable and authoritarian. Nevertheless, they are less likely to play interpersonal games and more likely to speak the truth.

Whatever the reason, loneliness is common. It is difficult to love someone who is absent. The challenge is to discover transcendent love: to love people, life, and God in both their absence and presence. As we discovered in mid-life, we do not depend totally or even primarily on people, but on God as our sustaining Ground of Life.

Most important is to love and be loved by God. God's love is always our saving grace especially when no humans directly love us. Our ultimate dependency on God culminates in the elderly years. No matter what our physical, social, and psychological conditions may be, God offers us life. Growing older in love enables us to depend on and enjoy the Spirit of life.

Those who have not known love may be horrified. Loneliness has caught them. If they have only learned to adjust to each other, but failed to grow in community, they will feel lost and empty in the absence of love. No further escape is possible. The demand of life: to love, screams out at them. It is their final hope—their final summons to live a life of love —to journey to the Promised Land.

Another difficulty that the elderly must face is the significant difference that often lies between the expectations and the realities of retirement. For example, we expect to live more fully in retirement, but socioeconomic problems impede our reaching our goals. Some of us never prepare for retirement and falsely assume that things will work out. Rather than dying of boredom, we can help ourselves by preparing now for the years that are left. We can walk through the desert of old age, accept its purifying teaching, and emerge renewed.

How we have lived in the past promises to be either a major obstacle or an aid to living through the elderly years. Those of us who have led normally mad lives have difficulty becoming old and happy. Our crisis will probably fracture our madness and call attention to what we have missed. In fact, normal madness makes little sense in the elderly years if only because it seldom pays dividends. Playing games in the face of death is indeed tragic.

Another obstacle to growth is the prejudice against being old—ageism. This cultural force can engender loneliness as well as feelings of worthlessness. A culture that judges people on their production rate surely sees little of the transcendent value in the elderly. Since the culture has nothing to learn from the elderly, and sees no value in them, they are a problem to be dealt with, a people who need to be treated and controlled. To transcend the cultural barbarism of ageism, faith in self and God are important. Loving God leads to an acceptance and compassion for all people, even those who violate or forget the elderly. To be able to say yes no matter what and to see meaning in the midst of oppression are redemptive processes. The primary focus, however, must be spiritual. Without the spiritual, the elderly become worthless and burdensome, and we lose our most valuable resource.

Embracing death is a redemptive force. When death embraces us, we return the embrace. Such communion evokes an enormous sense of power and vision that no one can take from us. When we accept death, nothing else can harm us. In dying, we destroy death and restore life.

The elderly years bring the milestones of retirement, being together with spouse or community in a new way, and children who make us "grand" parents, aunts, uncles, and friends. Being members of the oldest generation brings new limits and possibilities, new oppression and opportunity. It renews our way of living which places less emphasis on the functional, but does open new horizons, new visions, new words, new feelings, new life.

Our final dark night enlightens us and fills us with hope. This is our last Lent before we come to our eternal Easter. If we have run from life till now, this final Lent can be a saving grace that leads to resurrection. We must be patient: willing to wait and suffer in love, to stay in the desert rather than seek to escape it; otherwise, we may die without being redeemed. We must believe that life presents us with fasts, Advents, and Lents that promise feasts, Christmases, and Easters.

LAND OF LIFE

After the desert of old age, which may be either a devastating or a relatively easy and familiar journey, we settle down for the last time. Whether or not these relatively short or long years are meaningful is certainly influenced by social, economic, medical, and other environmental factors, but the paramount factor is spiritual. Even in the midst of poverty and oppression, we can live with dignity and integrity.

We increase our worth in experiencing ourselves as infinitely greater than our total successes, problems, pleasures, pains. Experiencing the Infinite within us, our dignity touches people. Our vision of the Infinite makes a concrete impact. Too often, however, people are intimidated by our power. Thus they minimize our value rather than accept it and benefit from it. They try to cover our power and repress or oppress it. Or more likely, they respond to our ills and deficits and neglect our help and assets.

We can break through the false myth that old age is meaningless and horrible. In spite of disease or economic oppression, we can be happier than anyone else. Rather than succumbing to a premature death or identifying life with physical activity or functional success, we can spiritually dance and laugh with life. We see through the normal madness of ageism, we are compassionate and forgiving with its proponents.

Looking back on life, we can say that we have run the good race, that we have given our best. Rather than empty desolation, life is fulfilling and consoling. Even though we are surrounded by the absence of loved ones, we feel present to them in their absence. Out there beyond our reach, we still touch and are touched. Indeed, we transcend our limits and go beyond the surface by constantly experiencing the ground of our being. Wherever and whenever we look, we see the Spirit of life.

The elderly years bring an appreciation of how easy it could have been to be seduced by the counterfeits of the Spirit. We understand the pressure put on people to be normally mad, but we realize that pleasure and success are only temporary fulfillments that do not last. We see that the mania for having offers sparse profit as compared to the treasure of being. Even though our search for the Spirit was frequently detoured, the Spirit never left us. The essense of life, the Holy Spirit, was and is always with us. We now have a pure vision of the essence of life, and being in the presence of the Holy Spirit enables us to rest in peace.

In old age we can look back with a compassionate smile at our attempts to be absolutely fulfilled. We know now that absolute satisfaction and enjoyment are never possible and ultimately inconsequential. Life always incorporates unfulfillment, discontent, unhappiness, misery, and pain along with fulfillment, joy, and pleasure. We let go of false promises of being filled once and for all and bear with joy the process of becoming.

Earth is a journey to heaven. While moments of heaven are experienced on earth, absolute fulfillment only comes after we finally stop dying and finally live forever. Nevertheless, in the elderly years we can feel more fulfillment, closer to eternal life, and nearer to the Kingdom of God. Rather than feeling wiped out, we feel we are returning to home. Realizing that all of life has been a search for old age, we look back with gratitude, we affirm the future, and feel consoled in the present.

We really become childlike, which is not a childish regression to an earlier stage of development. We can foster the open simplicity of an innocent child and the depth of a wise old sage. We look at reality and see more than the ordinary. Like the child, we play with life and celebrate every day. We live with a sense of surprise and exploration.

Love permeates life, and though there may be few people near or with us, we are in love. We live in love.

Despite environmental deprivation, an inner peace resides in the core of our being when we rest in love. Nothing much is foreign, for all life is familiar. Rather than being restless, jumpy, and lost, we feel that soon we will be home to rest eternally in love. However, those of us who have run from the desert will have a very difficult time believing in the promised land of love. Love's substitutes of success, pleasure, social recognition, and psychological adjustment only end in desolation.

More than any other time the elderly years call for transcendent autonomy. It is easy to play the game of being old: being passive, dependent, and burdensome. We can abdicate our authority rather than claim our life in the Infinite. Authentic autonomy is rooted in our spiritual life. Therefore it is possible to reach the zenith of autonomy even though we are dependent physically and socially. We can be free in a concentration camp, in a warehouse for old people, or in a rejecting community.

In spite of physical, social, and economic dependence, we can be truly independent. If we have grown throughout life in the Spirit of freedom, our elderly years culminate in self-determination. Our autonomy is based on being ultimately dependent on God. Paradoxically, the highest form of autonomy is rooted in and sustained by dependence, for we affirm our original and perpetual reliance on God.

Some of us become more active than ever before. We may join senior citizens clubs which offer opportunities for recreation and travel at a relatively low fee. Furthermore, we are invited to enjoy everyday living such as eating, sleeping, walking, and talking. The elderly often relive their life in dreams, so that sleep becomes an enjoyable experience. The elderly years offer more opportunities to do nothing rather than something, to enjoy the useless rather than the useful, to live in community rather than simply managing to cope. But if we have run from life, our dreams may become nightmares, and past forms of play that served as escapes prove to be futile. Over-drinking and overeating are practically fatal. The cri-sis of the elderly years calls for authentic play—a play filled with spirit.

The journey is nearing its end. The process of dying will soon cease; living will soon be permanent. We feel permanence is on its way, that nothing tem-porary lasts, that all temporary things call for the permanent. Seeing the permanent emerging on the horizon and coming closer gives us a vision that we never had so clearly before, a vision that helps us accept life and claim the future.

Without spirituality, life becomes at best gloomy and at worst meaningless. If primary meaning comes from being in good physical health, achieving func-tional success, or feeling in a state of contentment, then life eventually becomes absurd. Such a life becomes a constant escape from death, resurrection, and reconciliation. Especially in old age, when physi-cal and social maladies are more painful and con-stant, life dissipates without a spiritual vision. With-out Spirit, there is no life.

One who has escaped the challenges to grow throughout life is more likely to suffer mental illness or attempt suicide in the elderly years. Mental illness at this time is usually due to social isolation or organic impairment. Those who enter their seventies only to discover that life has been a charade can easily de-spair. In fact, suicide reaches its maximum rate for males between ages seventy-five and eighty-four. If we are accustomed to use money as an escape from spiritual questions, we may find at last it doesn't work. Finally we all have to face the radical issues of life and death.

Some of us see aged as worn-out, nonproductive, accident prone, worthless, and hard to live with. Others take a more positive view of the elderly as worthwhile and worthy of respect. How we see them determines to a high degree how we treat them. Although we may "talk" about the elderly in positive terms, we must honestly ask how we concretely behave toward them. Do we simply tolerate them, or do we care for and learn from them? Are "they" really one of "us"?

We usually feel uncomfortable when we think of sexuality in the elderly years. We make pathetic jokes about it or simply ignore it. The fact is that the elderly people can have an enjoyable sex life. When we practice sexuality as an art and integrate it with spirituality, it becomes satisfying and fulfilling. The quantity of genital relations invariably decreases as compared with the younger years, but the quality can increase. We should have more sexual know-how primarily from knowing each other better and being less likely to be sexist and ageist.

We continue to be more androgenous. Growing older together is becoming more alike, though never the same. Affectively we can reach out, touch, and communicate in innumerable ways. Actually, our sexuality leads more and more to a contemplative vision and appreciation of each other. Now a glance can convey a message of a lifetime and a promise of a future.

Our ideal is spirituality and sexuality to live in harmony so that we see the spiritual in the sexual and the sexual in the spiritual. Both these aspects of being human are interwoven and inseparable, so that to touch and to be touched is a sexual-spiritual act.

Our past attitudes and practices highly determine our sexual life in the latter years. If we integrate love and sexuality, we remain active and share a fulfilling relationship. However, a fragmented sexual life contributes nothing to the elderly years. A macho man who has identified sexuality with genitality will probably be impotent, and have no interest in incorporating female qualities into his life. A woman who has accepted the cultural expectation of becoming neuter in middle age will probably find herself "neuterized" in old age.

Love in the elderly years often takes on a fidelity that includes an asceticism to accept pain. To suffer for another's sake, such as in accepting social oppression, personal rejection, and general injustice, can be a clear and constant form of suffering love. To be sure, not all love involves pain; much love is quiet, gentle, and serene. Such love is accepted without complaining about it or wishing that it was taken away. We realize that pain is necessary for reconciling growth and that death will finally lead to painless living. Such redemptive love is based on our primary commitment to God, who gives us the courage and strength to love unconditionally.

Old men and women, however, can become irritable and angry. If they have repressed their anger and autonomy in the past, such bitter persons can be difficult to live with. The redemptive processes of suffering love and compassion are severely tested by miserable old people who seem to try to make everyone else miserable. Our ministry is to rekindle their hidden spirit and affirm our being together in the Spirit.

Living in the Spirit, many elderly people manifest a childlikeness, an open simplicity, a purity of the heart. Perhaps this is one reason why old people often play with children, and children often respond to them more openly than with other adults. Another reason may be that elderly people are less likely to be phony and to engage in interpersonal madness, but are more likely to play with a light and warm spirit that manifests festive love. They appreciate the humor of existence and laugh with life.

An exciting feature of old age is that there is more time to play. The spirit of play beckons us in our elderly years. If we have run from play all our life, the playful spirit may frighten us to death. Since we tend to choose activities that are most consistent with our past values and patterns, how we prepare for play is important. If we have played consistently and authentically throughout life, play is a welcome activity that becomes a light celebration of life. Without playful spirit, we are usually sad and empty. Dancing with the spirit of play, however, makes us gentle and happy.

Our final milestone is death. For the last time, death beckons us to live. To say yes to life means that life has been meaningful. If life has been an escape from death, then death can be devastating and absolute. Death is the end; there is no resurrection.

It is good to remember that we are always on our deathbed. Thinking of ourselves in our last moments can bring life into perspective. In spite of our limitations and sins, can we say that we are living a life of love? Despite all imperfections, phoniness, vices, can we say that we have tried to do the best we can? Can we say that we have journeyed through the deserts as well as through the promised lands? Though we may have been tempted to escape and even escaped temporarily, have we always come back to weather the storms? Can we say that we have never intentionally manipulated or exploited people? Can we say that we have never purposely violated life? If we did, can we say that we have repented and have been reconciled? Even though we may have had crippled feet, have we continued to dance with life?

Persons who have grown with death find it relatively easy to face death. Death is no stranger. Still, it is not entirely comfortable, for death is a powerful force that throws us back to our beginnings, an unknown and uncontrollable reality that cuts through all of life. Thus, to be afraid of death is normal, but to have the courage to face the dread of death evokes life.

If we have escaped from the desert, we will have difficult times coming to the promised land. And yet the final desert calls one last time for the journey to the Promised Land. A denial of death, a repression of painful feelings like depression and loneliness, and the identification of life with function are always key internal obstacles.

The cultural madness of ageism, our tendency to adore youth, militates against appreciating and fostering significant meaning in the elderly years. Old age becomes worthless rather than invaluable. A crucial danger is that elderly people themselves incorporate this cultural oppression and try to fulfill a false prophecy—that death is the end rather than the beginning of life.

"We" perpetuate ageism by assuring that "they"—the elderly people—are powerless, weak, dependent, and perhaps worthless. And medically, economically, and functionally many may fit this syndrome. But in other ways, and especially spiritually, they can be powerful, strong, independent, and full of worth. In fact, a paradoxical and uneasy saving grace is that happy elderly people intimidate "us"—those who are not elderly.

Their being so close to death threatens us, and reacting in defense, we control and oppress them. Consequently, rather than learning from them, we teach them. Rather than listening, we talk about them and to them. Rather than caring for them, we treat them.

They intimidate us by exposing our unauthentic lives, they summon us to question our values. Because they intimidate us, we try to put them into categories—to make them all the same—"typical" of old age. And even though we may not put many of them in geriatric facilities, we do minimize their value. Maybe these so-called old, weak, and power-less people can teach us something. Particularly those who are happy being useless and who promote different values can indict our obsession with work, power, and success.

Consider, for example, how old people intimidate us by questioning our quasi-living. Too often we as-sume that we can live without death. We delude ourselves into thinking that death will someday hap-pen rather than realizing that death is always hap-pening to us—not only to them. Since we are in fact beings-toward-death, we share their coming to death. Being close to death, elderly people proclaim the meaning of life. Rather than being intimidated, we can listen to them and let them help us. We can take the challenge and make the leap into being. We can help ourselves by letting the elderly help us.

Old people can help us by refusing to play the game of being old—dependent, silent, and worthless. They must proclaim themselves rather than silence their truth. They must encounter us and even con-front our normal madness. Rather than hiding from us, they must let themselves be seen.

Elderly persons can also accept us and be compas-sionate. Warriors who know what it means to battle life can help us bear the burden of existence and the weight of living authentically. And they can inspire us to seek what is best rather than settle for anything less. They can also expect us to show them justice and respect. They can be friends who help us to grow old and face death. They can advise us on what to expect, how to cope, and how to transcend as well as advise us on economic, social, and interpersonal and personal matters. Most of all, they can be our mentors in spirituality.

We can also help them. Rather than denying death, we can face death in ourselves and therefore in them. We can come to the turning point when we no longer are intimidated but can listen to them. Becoming more aware of our own living and dying, we can journey with them on their last trip. We can help them see and affirm in themselves that death is the final step in growth.

But are we really open to them? Or do we subtly hide from them? For example, at a social gathering do we talk to them for a few minutes, pat them on the head, and excuse ourselves, only returning when they need something? Instead of treating them as children, can we see that we sit on their shoulders? Can we truly love them? Can we show genuine hospitality wherein we give them the space and time to be themselves? Are we for them?

Can we become reconciled with the elderly, especially with those who have hurt us? Can we forgive —a giving that is always there with no strings attached? Do we give them projects to keep them happy rather than share happiness with them? Do we motivate and challenge rather than reinforce their dependency? Do we invite them to be interindependent? Do we ask for their help?

Do we show delight with the elderly? Rather than being irritated with them, do we see them as one of us and show genuine care and concern? How often do we have genuine fun with them, celebrate with them, and truly enjoy them? Or is being with them a routine, a way of being nice or of relieving our guilt? Do we condescend in our care? Can we truly listen to them? Do we get a kick out of them? Do we realize that the elderly are an infinite source of faith, love, and hope?

So what if some do tell the same story several times, they never tell it in the same way. The information is not the primary factor, but rather the sharing and being with. Though communication is helpful, communion is infinitely more important. Can we truly take in, support, and affirm the gift of their being? Rather than being resentful, can we be thankful that they are alive?

Can we show patience—a suffering and waiting in love? Can we move at their pace? Can we listen to their rhythm rather than force them to step to ours?

Do we understand old people? Can we enter into their world and appreciate their lives? Or do we analyze and manipulate them? Do we see them as a problem to handle rather than a mystery to appreciate? Do we take the elderly for granted rather than have a deep sense of gratitude?

A paramount point is to face and heal the "we-them" dichotomy. Rather than being against each other, we can come together. We can affirm our common ground and become members of the same humankind.

We need not propose a theory to justify being together, but rather we have to admit that our essential reality is being together. It is an old reality that must be rediscovered, rekindled, and lived. Whether or not we admit it, we have always shared in the same life-force and depended on its power. We can affirm that we are bound together by the Spirit of life. We can rejoice in standing on the same ground. We can grow older together in God's love.

BIBLIOGRAPHY

Bednarik, Karl. *The Male in Crisis.* Tr. Helen Sebba. Alfred A. Knopf, 1970.

Bernard, Harold W. *Human Development in Western Culture.* 5th ed. Allyn & Bacon, 1978.

Bier, William C. (ed.). *Aging: Its Challenge to the Individual and to Society.* Fordham University Press, 1975.

Bischof, Ledford J. *Adult Psychology.* 2d ed. Harper & Row, 1976.

Bühler, Charlotte. "The Course of Humans on a Psychological Problem." In W. R. Looft (ed.), *Developmental Psychology: A Book of Readings.* Holt, Rinehart, & Winston, 1972.

Butler, Robert N. *Why Survive? Being Old in America.* Harper & Row, 1975.

Cummings, Charles. *Spirituality and the Desert Experience.* Dimension Books, 1978.

Dangott, Lillian R., and Kalish, Richard A. *A Time to Enjoy: The Pleasures of Aging.* Prentice-Hall, 1979.

Eisendorf, Carl, and Lauton, M. Powell (eds.). *A Psychology of Adult Development and Aging.* Washington, D.C.: American Psychological Association, 1973.

Erikson, Erik H. *Identity: Youth and Crisis.* W. W. Norton & Co., 1968.

————. *Insight and Responsibility.* W. W. Norton & Co., 1964.

Fleming, David A. (ed.). *The Fire and the Cloud: An Anthology of Catholic Spirituality.* Paulist Press, 1978.

Goldberg, Stella R., and Deutsch, Francine. *Life-Span Individual and Family Development.* Brooks/Cole Publishing Co., 1977.

Gould, Roger L. *Transformations.* Simon & Schuster, 1979.

Gregory of Nyssa. *From Glory to Glory.* Ed. Jean Danielou. Tr. Kieran Kavanaugh and Otilio Rodriguez. ICS Publications, 1973.

Hammarskjöld, Dag. *Markings.* Tr. Leif Sjöberg and W. H. Auden. Alfred A. Knopf, 1964.

Heidegger, Martin. *Being and Time.* Tr. John Macquarrie and Edward Robinson. Harper & Row, 1962.

Hendricks, Jon, and Hendricks, C. Davis. *Aging in Mass Society: Myths and Realities.* Winthrop Publishers, 1977.

Hulicka, Irene M. (ed.). *Empirical Studies in the Psychology and Sociology of Aging.* Thomas Y. Crowell Co., 1977.

Huyck, Margaret Hellie. *Growing Older.* Prentice-Hall, 1974.

John of the Cross, St. *The Collected Works of St. John of the Cross.* Tr. Kieran Kavanaugh and Otilio Rodriguez. ICS Publications, 1973.

Johnston, William (ed.). *The Cloud of Unknowing and the Book of Privy Counseling.* Doubleday & Co., 1973.

Jones, Christopher. *Scott: A Meditation on Suffering and Helplessness.* Templegate Publishers, 1978.

Jung, Carl G. *Modern Man in Search of a Soul.* Tr. C. F. Baynes. Harcourt, Brace & Co., 1955.

Kalish, Richard A. *Late Adulthood: Perspectives on Human Development.* Brooks/Cole Publishing Co., 1975.

Kennedy, Carroll E. *Human Development: The Adult Years and Aging.* Macmillan Publishing Co., 1978.

Kimmel, Douglas C. *Adulthood and Aging.* John Wiley & Sons, 1974.

Kraft, William F. "Emergence and Formation in Adulthood." *Review for Religious,* Vol. 38, No. 3 (May 1979).

————. *Normal Modes of Madness.* Alba House, 1978.

————. "Nothingness and Psychospiritual Growth." *Review for Religious,* Vol. 37, No. 6 (Nov. 1978).

————. *A Psychology of Nothingness.* Westminster Press, 1974.

————. *The Search for the Holy.* Westminster Press, 1971.

Kübler-Ross, Elisabeth. *Death: The Final Stage of Growth.* Prentice-Hall, 1975.

————. *On Death and Dying.* Macmillan Co., 1969.

————. *Questions and Answers on Death and Dying.* Macmillan Publishing Co., 1974.

Levinson, Daniel J., et al. *The Seasons of a Man's Life.* Alfred A. Knopf, 1978.

Lidz, Theodore. *The Person: His and Her Development Throughout the Life Cycle.* Rev. 2d ed. Basic Books, 1976.

Lugo, James O., and Hershey, Gerald L. *Human Development: A Psychological, Biological and Sociological Approach to the Life Span.* 2d ed. Macmillan Publishing Co., 1979.

Mayer, Nancy. *The Male Mid-Life Crisis: Fresh Starts After Forty.* Doubleday & Co., 1978.

Merton, Thomas. *Contemplative Prayer.* Doubleday & Co., 1971.

Munroe, Robert L. and Ruth H. *Cross-Cultural Human Development.* Brooks/Cole Publishing Co., 1975.

Neugarten, Bernice L. (ed.). *Middle Age and Aging.* University of Chicago Press, 1968.

Newman, Barbara M., and Newman, Philip R. *Development Through Life.* Rev. ed. Dorsey Press, 1979.

Nouwen, Henri J. M. *The Wounded Healer: Ministry in Contemporary Society.* Doubleday & Co., 1972.

O'Collins, Gerald. *The Second Journey: Spiritual Awareness and the Mid-Life Crisis.* Paulist Press, 1978.

Palmore, Erdman (ed.). *Normal Aging 2: Reports from the Duke Longitudinal Study.* Duke University Press, 1974.

Puner, Morton. *To the Good Long Life: What We Know About Growing Old.* Universe Books, 1974.

Rahner, Karl. *On the Theology of Death.* Tr. Charles H. Henkey. Herder & Herder, 1961.

Schell, Robert E., and Hall, Elizabeth. *Developmental Psychology Today.* 3d ed. CRM Books, Random House, 1979.

Schlossberg, Nancy K., and Entine, Alan D. (eds.). *Counseling Adults.* Brooks/Cole Publishing Co., 1977.

Sheehy, Gail. *Passages: Predictable Crises of Adult Life.* E. P. Dutton & Co., 1974.

Smith, Bert K. *Aging in America.* Beacon Press, 1973.

Solnick, Robert L. *Sexuality and Aging.* Rev. ed. University of California Press, 1978.

Stevens-Long, Judith. *Adult Life: Developmental Processes.* Mayfield Publishing Co., 1979.

Streng, Frederick J.; Lloyd, Charles L.; and Allen, Jay T. (eds.). *Ways of Being Religious: Readings for a New Approach to Religion.* Prentice-Hall, 1973.

Taylor, John V. *The Go-Between God.* Fortress Press, 1973.

Teresa of Avila. *The Interior Castle.* Tr. Kieran Kavanaugh and Otilio Rodriguez. Paulist Press, 1979.

Troll, Lillian E. *Early and Middle Adulthood.* Brooks/Cole Publishing Co., 1975.

Underhill, Evelyn. *Mysticism: A Study in the Nature and Development of Man's Spiritual Consciousness.* E. P. Dutton & Co., 1911.

Vaillant, George E. *Adaptation to Life.* Little, Brown & Co., 1977.

Van Kaam, Adrian. *The Transcendent Self: The Formative Spirituality of Middle, Early and Later Years of Life.* Dimension Books, 1979.

Weil, Simone. *Waiting for God.* Tr. Emma Crufurd. Harper & Row, Colophon Books, 1973.

Whitehead, Evelyn E., and Whitehead, James D. *Christian Life Patterns: The Psychological Challenges and Religious Invitations of Adult Life.* Doubleday & Co., 1979.